The

What is the extraordinary appeal of Elinor M. Brent-Dyer's Chalet School, that it should generate so much interest in so many people? The fans range in age from eight to eighty, and the quantity of letters received by the fan clubs and by the publishers testifies to the Chalet School's enduring popularity.

This book (which includes material from *Elinor M. Brent-Dyer's Chalet School*) is an attempt to answer the thousands of questions that are asked about the Chalet School and about Elinor Brent Dyer, who was born a hundred years ago, in 1894. Helen McClelland, acknowledged Chalet School expert and patron of The Friends of the Chalet School, has not only brought Elinor back to life in fascinating detail but has also described the history of the Chalet School (not forgetting the stalwarts on the Staff!), given details of Joey's remarkable family, and discovered possible locations for the various School sites in Austria, Guernsey, Hereford, Wales and Switzerland.

Amongst the articles are two Chalet School short stories, never before published in paperback.

The Chalet School
Companion

The Chalet School
Companion

Helen McClelland

Armada
An Imprint of HarperCollins*Publishers*

First published in Great Britain in Armada 1994

1 3 5 7 9 10 8 6 4 2

Armada is an imprint of HarperCollins Children's Books,
a division of HarperCollins Publishers Ltd,
77/85 Fulham Palace Road, Hammersmith,
London W6 8JB

Copyright © Helen McClelland 1994

The author asserts the moral right to be
identified as the author of this work.

ISBN 0 00 674911-9

Printed and bound in Great Britain by
HarperCollins Manufacturing, Glasgow

Conditions of Sale
This book is sold subject to the condition that it shall not, by
way of trade or otherwise, be lent, re-sold, hired out or
otherwise circulated without the publisher's prior consent in
any form of binding or cover other than that in which it is
published and without a similar condition including this
condition being imposed on the subsequent purchaser.

Contents

INTRODUCTION

Elinor Brent-Dyer's Chalet School has been flourishing for nearly seventy years. Today's enthusiastic readers could be, and sometimes are, the grandchildren of those who enjoyed the books when they first appeared, and the Chalet School paperbacks continue to sell at an astonishing rate.

Why should these particular books have retained their popularity in such a remarkable way? Perhaps the kind of inbuilt momentum that might be called the series factor has played its part. But there were other popular series of children's books, both comparable and contemporary with the Chalet stories, and most of these have now disappeared. So why were the Chalet School books among the few that resisted the downward trend? Why are they now virtually the only survivors from the pre-war golden age of the school story that are still regularly bought and widely read today, and by both children and adults? What kind of people are they who become Chalet School fans today, in the 1990s? Their number and enthusiasm are beyond question: not only do they buy up thousands of paperbacks and scour the secondhand market for out-of-print hardbacks, they even devote time to writing fan letters – letters which continue to this day to flow in a steady stream from around the world. Very often these letters ask questions about Elinor Brent-Dyer, seeking in particular to learn where she got the idea for her amazingly successful series.

This last question is easier to answer than some of the others. Elinor, in 1924, had spent a long and enjoyable holiday in the Austrian Tirol and had decided on her return to use Austria as the setting for a school story "with a difference". The book that grew from her idea was *The School at the Chalet*, and it was published in October 1925 by the Scottish firm W. & R. Chambers (one of the leading publishers of school stories at that time).

Many of the places Elinor had visited during her holiday are described in the early Chalet School books, and can be identified without much difficulty. For the Chalet School's original Tirolean location at "Briesau" on the shores of the "Tiernsee" really does exist, complete with the little mountain railway, the lake steamers, and other features of the district made familiar by the stories. But in real life the village of "Briesau" has another name, as do both the lake itself and the town at the foot of the mountains which is the starting point for the little cog-wheel train (see Locations).

The School at the Chalet was not Elinor Brent-Dyer's first book. Some years before her visit to Austria she had become friendly with a theatrical husband-and-wife team, Edith and Julian Bainbridge, who at this time were running a small repertory theatre in the town where Elinor lived. Hazel, the Bainbridges' ten-year-old daughter, was a talented child actress, and she and Elinor were to become great friends despite the wide difference in their ages (Elinor was twenty-seven). One of the things that Hazel most enjoyed was listening to all the wonderful stories that Elinor could tell. And it was specially for Hazel that Elinor wrote *Gerry Goes to School*, her first published book. She was devoted to Hazel, whom she often called her little "adopted sister" – the same phrase Joey uses in the books about Robin Humphries. So possibly the character of "the Robin", though not directly a portrait, may owe something to Hazel.

Until recently, Hazel Bainbridge was still active in the theatre (and her daughters, Kate O'Mara and Belinda Carroll, are both well-known actresses). But present-day readers are unlikely to come across *Gerry Goes to School*, because it and the six other books belonging to a set known as the "La Rochelle" series have been out of print for many years. However, these books do survive in a link with the Chalet School, because many of the characters from "La Rochelle" appear later in the Chalet series (see Questions).

Elinor followed *Gerry* with two other books, one being *The Maids of La Rochelle*, the first of her Channel Islands stories. All three enjoyed a moderate success. But no one could possibly have foreseen in October 1925, when *The School at the Chalet* first appeared, just how widely and enduringly popular this book (with, later, its multitude of successors) was going to prove. Nor could the author have had the remotest inkling that she had set off, that

October, along a road that would continue for the next forty-four years, ending only with her death in September 1969. During that time, the Chalet series was to reach the staggering total of fifty-eight full length hardback books and one shorter paperback (see Questions) and the stories were to gain a wide and faithful following. Quantities of fan mail would arrive from many distant parts of the English-speaking world as well as from Chalet enthusiasts all over Britain. Elinor would make frequent appearances at book exhibitions up and down the country, and be interviewed in the *Tonight* programme on television. There would even be a Chalet School Club – something unique in the history of the girls' school story: this ran successfully from May 1959 until after Elinor Brent-Dyer's death some ten years later, its membership then numbering nearly 4000 fans. Today, a further twenty-five years on, the club has a number of successors, both in Britain and overseas – a remarkable tribute to the Chalet School's continuing vitality (see Chalet Fans, Past and Present).

How odd to think that at the time of her visit to the Tirol Elinor was just an unknown schoolteacher who happened to choose Austria for her long summer holiday. But it was Austria that provided the well-loved and different setting that comes high on the list when fans are asked their reasons for enjoying the stories. Elinor's "Briesau-am-Tiernsee" had caught her readers' imaginations not only because of its beauty but because it was fun. What girl would not prefer to forsake the ordinary bus or suburban train and travel to school by that "quaint little mountain railway", and then in the "little white steamer" across the sapphire-blue lake, with breath-taking views on every side?

In this delightful setting the most ordinary school activities – walks, for instance – can seem glamorous; while the extraordinary adventures – two girls getting lost in the mist on a mountain precipice, or the Chalet being engulfed by floods during the spring thaw – appear credible, given the school's Alpine situation. And everything else about the school was different too – the mixture of nationalities, and religious denominations, the near-family atmosphere (at least in the early books) and the delicious-sounding meals.

Another facet of the books that appealed to fans was mentioned by a schoolgirl, who wrote to Elinor that "in reading the French conversation of the Chalet girls, unknowingly I learnt quite a few words, phrases and idioms . . .", and although Elinor's own knowledge of French and German was apparently limited (she sometimes makes glaring errors in both languages!) many readers would agree on this point.

But it is plain that, had there been no more to the books than a glamorous background and a lot of instruction, more or less attractively packaged (as one grown-up fan said, "So many interesting histori-cal and geographical facts which the reader can painlessly absorb"), then the Chalet series would long ago have been forgotten – like so many other school stories. Certainly the stories' picturesque locations – not only in Austria, but in the Channel Islands, Herefordshire, Wales, and Switzerland –

have helped; but this aspect is probably less important today than it was originally, for now holidays abroad have become almost the norm, and this may rob the books of some of their former novelty. That the Chalet School continues to survive after nearly seventy years is mainly a tribute to the entertaining stories, the sense of comedy and fun, and above all to the characterisation shown in the early books. Here, the pupils are neither the paragons of virtue nor the monsters of depravity that are found in some school stories, but credible schoolgirls, who may have a rather unusual number of adventures but still manage to behave and talk like human beings.

In fact, Elinor's principal achievement would seem to lie in having created at the beginning of her series, where it mattered most, a set of characters who gradually assumed an almost independent existence in her eyes and those of her readers. Then, by employing various devices, she was able to keep at least the most important of these characters on stage throughout the series. Later, their multitudinous children were to follow in their footsteps at the school, often learning from the same teachers as had their parents.

Nor was it only the Chalet School characters that began to seem real. Just as important for the readers was their belief in the Chalet School itself, as an abiding institution whose customs may gradually evolve but whose traditions remain constant throughout the series. Maybe it was only a few fans who actually wrote and asked the publishers to send prospectuses of the school. But many keen readers could recite from memory the Chalet School's constitution and rules, could explain the timetable, and take on the "sheepdog" duties of guiding a new girl round the school. Most things remain comfortingly the same: the pattern of days for speaking English, French or German; the Christmas play and the half-term excursions; the rituals of prep and meals, even the mundane things like the dormitory curtains and that splendid all-purpose article of furniture – a combined dressing-table/desk and chest-of-drawers – that is always there, along with the inevitable "plumeau", in every cubicle, term after term, book after book.

Plenty of reasons, then, to show why readers, once hooked, will often begin to feel (as Joey did) that "the Chalet School must go on". Probably the readers themselves would not be able to explain what it is in the books that has turned them into addicts, but perhaps just one person's experience may give a clue: "Apart from some of the expressions they use, like 'top-hole', I always think of the Chalet School as happening today."

THE LONG ROAD TO
THE CHALET SCHOOL

The life story of Elinor Brent-Dyer

Part One – *Early Life*

Not for Elinor Brent-Dyer the glorious mountains of the Tirol as a scenic backdrop to her childhood. The Chalet School's author was born and grew up in South Shields – an industrial town in Tyneside, which in those turn-of-the-century days was among the liveliest ship-building centres in the North-East but was hardly a glamorous place. Nor could No. 52 Winchester Street, the house where Elinor was born on 6th April 1894 and lived during the first nineteen years of her life, have been described as either high class or elegant. It was a respectable but very ordinary red-brick terraced house, dating from the 1870s, with a fair number of rooms but no bathroom, no running hot water or inside lavatory (not unusual for those days), and no garden, only a smallish back yard. Nothing like the gracious homes inhabited by the Maynards and the Russells.

Nor was it only in material circumstances that Elinor's childhood background differed from those of her fictional characters. In all her books Elinor shows a particular fondness for describing large happily united families, but she herself was one of only two children and she came from a broken home.

Her parents' marriage had been short-lived, and there are indications that a lack of harmony existed from quite early on. Certainly the couple were very different in both character and family background. Charles Dyer, Elinor's father, was an extrovert, and bohemian in tastes; his wife, Nelly, was by temperament and upbringing conventional. Nelly came from a well-known and respected local family with deep roots in the North-East. Charles was a native of Portsmouth (a city frequently mentioned in the early Chalet books) and a complete newcomer to Tyneside. He had originally served as an Engineer Officer in the Royal Navy but had been obliged to take early retirement following a bout of ill-health, and he had come to South Shields in the autumn of 1892 to work as a marine insurance surveyor.

The following spring, Charles and Nelly – or, to give both their full names, Charles Morris Brent Dyer and Eleanor Watson Rutherford – were married; the couple then set up house at 52 Winchester Street where Nelly had already been living since she was about six years old. Elinor was born a year later; and only fourteen months after that her brother, Henzell Watson Dyer, arrived on 25th June 1895. His unusual first name is of Huguenot origin and it had been a favourite name with his mother's family, the Rutherfords, for well over a hundred years.

The Winchester Street household included another important resident: Hannah Rutherford, Nelly

Dyer's widowed mother. Hannah was a woman of strong character, and she not only lived in the house, she was its legal owner and for many years had been accustomed to acting as head of the family. For Charles Dyer the situation must have been difficult.

In any case, things were not quite as they seemed at 52 Winchester Street. Outwardly the house appeared to contain a perfectly normal three-generation family: father, mother, two small children and a resident grandmother, with the occasional uncle or cousin staying for different lengths of time. But another person might by rights have expected to live with this household. Charles Dyer had been a widower at the time he married Elinor's mother and by his first marriage he had had a son, named Charles Arnold Lloyd Dyer. This little boy, barely five years old when his father married again, had spent the years after his mother's death in a pathetic kind of wandering passage between lodgings up and down the country, being for the most part left in the care of landladies. It is hard to think of any reason why poor Charles Arnold should not have come to live in South Shields with his father and stepmother once they had settled down after their marriage, for he had no other close relatives and there was ample room at 52 Winchester Street. The fact is, and this remains one of the mysteries in Elinor's background, that the child apparently never so much as visited the household. Odder still: among Elinor's surviving friends and relatives, not one seemed to recall ever hearing a word of Charles Arnold's existence.

But then neither were most people aware of the true situation when, one day in 1897, Charles Dyer took his departure from Winchester Street never to return. Elinor's mother and grandmother seem to have taken extraordinary pains to disguise the complete breakdown of the marriage, and somehow an impression spread around that Mrs Dyer was now a widow, having as the saying goes "lost her husband". And so in a way she had lost him, although Charles was not in fact to die until a further fourteen years after the legal separation took place.

At the time Elinor was barely three and Henzell not quite two. Both were too young to understand what was happening, but not too young to have noticed their father's continuing absence, and Elinor at least must have asked questions repeatedly. No one can tell today what answers she received. Nor is it known whether she and Henzell ever saw their father again. On balance it would seem unlikely they did, in view of the elaborate measures their mother had taken to make it appear Charles no longer existed. And unquestionably Mrs Dyer would not have informed her children when their father eventually set up house with another woman, by whom he later had a son and to whom he was to bequeath almost everything of which he died possessed.

As one result of all these smoke-screen operations, Elinor's early life took place against a curious background of secrecy and evasion. Little wonder that she grew up to be reticent, not to say secretive where her personal life was concerned, though always ready to hold forth about her fictional characters and on most other subjects as well.

A very early photograph of Elinor is quite revealing. It shows a very serious, rather wary and inward-looking little girl, with long straight fair hair, who appears to be about six years old. Not a very pretty little girl, it must be acknowledged: the heavy features and the large nose characteristic of Elinor in later life are already foreshadowed. Nor does she look very happy, but perhaps it is not surprising that the small Elinor should appear somewhat mournful, for the people close to her seemed to make a habit of disappearing.

First it was her father. And although no one can say how much Elinor knew about him even when she grew up, let alone how she felt, it could be significant that, when she chose a new form of surname to use as a writer, it was from her father that she took the name Brent, adding it with a hyphen to Dyer.

Next it had been her grandmother who vanished. In January 1901 Hannah Rutherford died, leaving a wide gap in the Winchester Street household where she had always wielded such a powerful influence. At this time Elinor was six and a half and Henzell only five; but, young as they were, it is unlikely that this was their first experience of a death in their immediate circle. The children of Elinor and Henzell's generation would often hear of death in their own age group, for at that period many serious and often fatal illnesses were still common which are almost unknown today: diphtheria, scarlet fever, smallpox and tuberculosis among them. The last-named used

19

then to cause many hundreds of deaths each year in South Shields alone. And one at least of these deaths was to affect Elinor closely.

A friend and contemporary of hers, named Elizabeth Jobling, lived in a house immediately opposite to the Dyers. For several years Elizabeth and Elinor attended the same school; and being near neighbours the two were companions on the mile-and-a-half-long walks between Winchester Street and Westoe Village where the school was situated. But Elizabeth was one of the many unfortunate people at that time who contracted tuberculosis; and at the early age of sixteen she died.

The effect of her death on Elinor can be imagined. And the following year, on 24th September 1912, Elinor was to suffer an even more shattering bereavement. With dramatic suddenness, her beloved brother, aged seventeen, was stricken with a fatal illness, cerebro-spinal meningitis, and was instantly taken into the local isolation hospital. Five days later he was dead. And this loss, coming as it did only a year after the death of her schoolfriend, was to leave a deep and permanent stamp on Elinor's personality. Henzell had been her earliest companion, and the two had been thrown very much together during those years when their mother, in her attempt to build a wall of respectability around the one-parent family, discouraged contact with the outside world. It had been Henzell who joined in the imaginary games that Elinor created from her earliest days; and it was to Henzell she had poured forth her first stories. To the end of her life, fifty-seven years after he died, Elinor would still be noting in her diary that 25th June was "Henzell's birthday". And although in later life she never talked about her brother to anyone outside her immediate circle, and seldom mentioned him even within it, it is clear that his memory always remained with her.

With Henzell's death all but one of the most important figures in Elinor's childhood had gone. Only her mother remained. And less than a year later Nelly Dyer, who was now genuinely a widow, was married to a Mr Septimus Ainsley, a man Elinor seems always to have disliked.

A new life now began for Elinor, bringing with it a new home. This was in one of the better-class residential districts of South Shields; and as a house it was vastly superior to her first home – in both comfort and social status. But with her mother's marriage, and the move from Winchester Street, the break-up of Elinor's original family circle was complete.

Part Two – *School Life*

School was to be a life-sentence in Elinor's case. For if her own school-days are added to the time she spent as student, pupil-teacher, teacher and finally as headmistress of her own school, the impressive total amounts to almost half a century. And this takes account only of real-life schools. Once her Chalet School was firmly established Elinor was never really to leave school until the day she died.

Her experience of schools was also wider and more varied than might be expected in view of the relatively narrow range of establishments portrayed in her books. She had become an "unqualified teacher" on her eighteenth birthday – 6th April, 1912; and during the next thirty-six years she taught in a variety of both state and private schools, small and large, working with boys as well as girls and with mixed classes. She attended training college for two years to obtain a teaching qualification; taught, at different times, English, history, Latin, and class singing, and also coached hockey and folk-dancing.

For a while she studied part-time at the Newcastle Conservatoire of Music, where she learnt piano, cello, and singing. She worked for five years as a private governess; and finally became headmistress of a school she founded in Hereford.

This long procession of schools begins in about 1900 when Elinor first became a pupil at St Nicholas's School, which in 1908 moved to Westoe Village, the most sought-after residential district in the whole area round South Shields.

St Nicholas's was a select private school with around fifty pupils, including a number of small boys in the kindergarten class (Elinor's brother spent a couple of years there). It was run by two formidable ladies, the Misses Alice and Henrietta Stewart, and significantly the school was always known locally not as St Nicholas's but as "The Misses Stewart's School". Here a strong emphasis was laid on the paramount importance of good manners and ladylike behaviour, while the teaching was possibly on the old-fashioned side even for the times. From Elinor's point of view this was hardly the right balance: she was a clever child who could have benefited from more high-powered academic teaching and it was not easy for her to assume a mantle of low-key refinement. From her father she had inherited a tendency to be outspoken and an extrovert temperament, quite different from her mother's more conformist personality; by nature she was full of enthusiasm and exuberance, was considered boisterous in behaviour as a child, and throughout her life had a rather loud voice, a hearty laugh, and a considerable disregard for conventions in dress and manner – decidedly not the qualities to make her a model pupil at the Misses Stewart's establishment. However, the school undoubtedly left its mark on her to some extent; for when grown-up Elinor did have at least a theoretical respect for the conventional patterns of ladylike behaviour, as well as a genuine belief in the importance of good manners: the latter emerges throughout her books, and frequently did in real life – as many of her former pupils would testify.

In complete contrast was her first experience of teaching, for Elinor went straight from "The Misses Stewart's" to work in a couple of the local Board Schools, as they were then known. Here she quickly gained a reputation for colourful eccentricity, which was to follow her into her student days (for example, she called herself "Patricia Maraquita" during her two years at the City of Leeds Training College) and right through her whole teaching career. Later on this included several more local authority schools and the well-respected Boys' High School in South Shields, independent schools in Middlesex and Hampshire, and even a short spell filling in at "The Misses Stewart's".

Last of all, after moving to Hereford in the 1930s, she set up her own school, the Margaret Roper School (named after Sir Thomas More's accomplished daughter). This real-life school, which ran from September 1938 to July 1948, shared many ideals and customs with the fictional Chalet School, and it too had a strong, though non-denominational, religious tradition. Many features of Chalet School life were to become familiar at the Margaret Roper School, among them, at various times, concerts, folk-dancing, pageants in the garden, exhibitions and sales of work, collections for charity, Girl Guides, expeditions to places of historical interest, school songs and plays, and in particular the annual Christmas play. This was always specially written by Elinor and was sometimes the very same play as the Chalet School girls were performing.

There were other resemblances, some deliberately contrived, some coincidental. For example, the Margaret Roper School had almost exactly the same uniform as the Chalet School, with brown and flame being the school colours. And the Hereford school even had its princesses among the pupils: their identity, like that of Elisaveta in *The Princess of the Chalet School*, was meant to be a secret, but in fact most people knew the children were the granddaughters of the Emperor Haile Selassie.

Many similarities existed, then, at least on paper. In hard cold fact there were just as many differences, and the Margaret Roper School was never to enjoy the phenomenal record of the Chalet School, although it was moderately successful for a number of years and undoubtedly filled a local need during the war. But Elinor, despite her gifts as a teacher, was not cut out to be a headmistress; and towards the end her interest in the real-life school rapidly faded, and became ever more fixed on the imaginary establishment.

All in all she was perhaps not really sorry when, in 1948, the Margaret Roper School finally closed its doors. At least she could now give her undivided attention to the Chalet School.

Part Three – *Book Life*

During the ten-year life of the Margaret Roper School Elinor had managed, in the midst of all her other commitments, to write and publish fourteen books. In the decade that followed, her output rose to the remarkable total of thirty-eight – sixteen of the books being completed within two years.

That tells much about the change in her circumstances. But it also confirms that Elinor's competence in the sheer mechanics of producing a book had been increasing steadily through the years. Not that her later books are superior in quality. On the contrary, most of her best stories belong to the early and middle years of her writing career. But undeniably she had in the course of time learnt many tricks of the trade.

Oddly enough, it had been getting started at all that gave Elinor the most trouble, despite the fact that she had been making up stories from the time when she first learnt to speak. Imaginary games and story-telling had indeed been her main occupations during the early years when she and her small brother had lived a somewhat isolated existence. And loneliness probably increased Elinor's natural tendency to create, and then take refuge in, an imaginary world. This in the future was to prove both an asset and a liability. As a writer it enabled her to believe completely and absolutely in her own fictional characters and their world, and to convey this conviction to her readers; as a person it sometimes made her not so much "economical with the truth" as over-elaborate and extravagant in embroidering it. But no one could deny that Elinor possessed a lively imagination, nor that she had great natural facility as a writer.

She could, it appears, both read and write by the time she was four. And the stories, which she had at first poured forth vocally to her little brother and anyone else who could be persuaded to listen, were soon to be untidily committed to paper (to the end of her life her manuscripts were amazingly messy!). And from this point on, Elinor, as described by many of her friends, "was always scribbling away". Not that she ceased to relate stories out loud: one of her younger schoolfellows recalled in a letter how Elinor would often enliven walks to the beach with her tales – "I can see her now, sitting on a rock telling us stories which I loved".

By her late teens Elinor had some reputation locally as an aspiring authoress; and already at this stage one or two of her stories had appeared in magazines and local newspapers. Even so, she did not enjoy quite the same precocious success as her Chalet School heroine, Jo Bettany, whose first book appears when she is only eighteen: Elinor was to be twenty-eight before *her* first book was accepted for publication.

This book, *Gerry Goes to School* (published by W. & R. Chambers in 1922, and a most important milestone in Elinor's career) was specially written for Hazel Bainbridge. Hazel's parents were running a small repertory theatre in South Shields at this time, and two plays written by Elinor were performed by their company. Neither play has survived, but unquestionably Elinor owed the start of her writing career to these plays and to the Bainbridges' encouragement. For despite her story-telling powers and facility in getting words on to paper, it seems that until this point she had never bothered to complete anything. As she explains in one of the Chalet Club Newsletters: ". . . I'd *begun* quite a number of books . . . but I always got tired of them and left them unfinished". The Bainbridges – with their offer to perform her plays, thus setting a deadline for completion – and above all their small daughter Hazel, who adored Elinor and always wanted to know what happened next in her stories – had provided exactly the stimulus that was required.

Once over that first hurdle in 1922 Elinor was never to look back. Less than a year later *Gerry* had a sequel, and in the following year Elinor took a further step forward with *The Maids of La Rochelle*, the first of her Guernsey stories. Here for the first time the setting plays an essential part in the story: *The Maids of La Rochelle* could hardly take place anywhere but in the Channel Islands, whereas in Elinor's first two books the events could happen almost anywhere. This book was also the first of Elinor's to be given favourable notices by the national press. But although the story marked another milestone, it was only a milestone. The really momentous turning-point in Elinor's writing career was to come with her visit to Austria in 1924.

Today no one can tell what her reasons were for choosing Austria as a holiday destination. At that time, with the Great War only five years in the past, the British more often chose France or Switzerland for their holidays. But the Tirol had one great advantage for the tourist: because the rate of inflation at this point had reached an almost unimaginable height, Austria was then a very cheap country for foreigners to visit. And this would have been a great attraction for Elinor who was not well off. Anyway, her reasons hardly matter. The important thing is that in the Tirol Elinor not only enjoyed the holiday of a lifetime but found the inspiration for a series that would become her life's work.

No written record of her holiday exists – or rather, no directly personal record. But anyone seeking to know how Elinor and the friend who was her companion spent their time, and where they went, has only to read the early Chalet School stories. In these books many of Elinor's descriptions could almost have come from the diary she never wrote. And the profusion of small everyday details, all presented with such obvious affection, help the reader to picture everything: the impressively beautiful scenery; the trips on the mountain railway and across the lake; the delicious meals; the mountain scrambles; the Tzigane bands playing outside the "Kron Prinz Karl" (today bands still perform on the terrace of its real-life equivalent); and so on . . . Whenever the Chalet girls make an expedition it seems that Elinor had been there before them; and her reactions to the places and to some of the people she met all play their part.

Immediately on returning from the Tirol to her teaching post in Hampshire Elinor got started on *The School at the Chalet*; and this book, which eventually would have fifty-eight successors, was published in October 1925. At its first appearance it was in a brown hardback edition, with a pictorial cover as well as a charming coloured dust-wrapper and four black and white illustrations by Nina K. Brisley (who was to provide illustrations for nearly half the series). The Chalet School was on the road.

From this point onwards Elinor was to continue producing books, and at an increasing rate, until the end of her life (the last of the Chalet series, *Prefects of the Chalet School*, was in fact published six months after she died). Altogether, during the forty-seven years spanning her writing career, her output was more than a hundred published books; there were also the "missing" Chalet School stories (see the section on Questions) and a number of unpublished manuscripts, including two collections of poems and a massive historical novel about Sir Thomas More and his family. Among the published books there are two series in addition to the Chalet School stories: "La Rochelle" (seven books) and "Chudleigh Hold" (three books), as well as several linked pairs of stories. There are fourteen books about schools other than the Chalet School, and one Girl Guide story; the remainder are family stories, adventure stories and historical tales.

All round not a bad achievement; especially bearing in mind that until she was fifty-four Elinor was obliged to continue working at least part-time as a teacher and could write only in the evenings or during the holidays.

But it all comes back to that holiday in Austria. It was this which gave birth to the Chalet School. And beyond any possible question it was the Chalet series that carried Elinor Brent-Dyer's name throughout Britain and into many far corners of the English-speaking world. Just as it is the Chalet books that are still keeping her name alive today, more than sixty years on.

Postscript – *The end of the story*

For a considerable period, from 1957, Elinor, who had always lived with her mother until her death that year, struggled to maintain the enormous Victorian villa that had housed her school. Eventually, towards the end of 1964, some friends succeeded in persuading her to sell up and move with them into a house at Redhill in Surrey.

Her health was now beginning to fail, and it seems that for the first time Elinor's hitherto inexhaustible vitality and enthusiasm were also flagging. But she was to continue with the Chalet books, five of which were produced during these last years at Redhill. And to the end of her life she does appear to have retained some enjoyment in her writing. It also undoubtedly gave her great pleasure to see the successful progress of her beloved Chalet School in the Armada paperback series.

Her death, when it came on 20 September 1969, was quite sudden and peaceful.

Elinor once replied, when asked about the future

of the Chalet books: "I can't say for I honestly don't know how long the series will continue. As long as I do myself, I hope."

At least that hope has been more than realised.

CHALET SCHOOL LOCATIONS

Part One – *The Tirolean Years*

When Elinor Brent-Dyer chose to spend her 1924 summer holiday in Austria this choice was to affect the whole future course of her life. For had she decided to go elsewhere that summer it is possible the Chalet School as such would never have existed, since it was undoubtedly Elinor's visit to Austria which started the whole enterprise, and her abiding affection for the Tirol that coloured her long-term approach to the stories.

At the beginning of the series Elinor had deliberately set out to disguise the school's exact location in the Tirol, and for many years she had succeeded in doing this by changing certain important place names and topographical details. It was not until the 1960s, some forty years after her visit, that she was willing to share the secret. And in the meantime most readers, searching vainly through maps and travel books for the name Briesau-am-Tiernsee, had concluded that the place must be imaginary. Only a handful of fans were lucky enough to stumble on an exciting discovery during their searches. Perhaps it was a familiar name like Scholastika that drew their attention to the Achensee, a lake high in the mountains above the Inn valley. A closer study of the Achensee district map would then quickly reveal many other well-known places: Buchau, Seespitz, Seehof, Gaisalm and Eben. In fact, as present-day readers can check for themselves, the only Chalet School name missing from the shores of the Achensee is that of Briesau itself; and the map makes it plain beyond doubt that the village called Pertisau *must* be the original Briesau. Its lakeside position on a triangular wedge of land running up into the mountains, and situated roughly halfway between Seespitz and Gaisalm, fits the stories exactly. And although another familiar name, that of the little town "Spärtz", does not appear on the map either, there is a town called Jenbach in precisely the right position at the foot of the mountains. In further confirmation, a cogwheel railway climbs the mountainside from Jenbach station to connect with the Achensee steamers at Seespitz. No question about it: Spärtz in real life is Jenbach, the Tiernsee is the Achensee, and Briesau Pertisau. The site of the Chalet School really does exist!

To reach the Achensee from outside Austria it is simplest to take a plane to Munich, and then a bus over the Achenpass and on to Pertisau – a beautiful journey and relatively quick. However, it is also possible to follow the old Chalet School route, the traditional way, and travel by boat and train. Once at Jenbach station, the refreshment-room across the

35

yard can be seen where, one Christmas, Herr Anserl treated Madge, Joey and the Robin to hot coffee and delicious rolls. There, too, is the delightful old-fashioned hotel, the Alte Toleranz, mentioned in several books (by no means so old-fashioned now!). And there at the end of the station platform is the Achenseebahn, the little mountain train that "carries you up to a height of three thousand feet and more above the sea level".

From here onwards, it is possible in imagination to accompany the Bettanys and Grizel Cochrane as they make their first ever trip to the Chalet School:

Higher and higher they climbed, now and then stopping at a tiny wayside station, till at last they reached the great Alp, or rather Alm, as they are called in the Tyrol; and there before them, dark, beautiful, and clear as a mirror, spread the Tiern [Achen] See, with its three tiny hamlets and two little villages round its shores; and towering round on all sides the mighty limestone crags and peaks of the mountains.

The railway terminus is known as Seespitz, and here the steamer was waiting for the passengers. Dick [Bettany] was there too, ready to help with the parcels.

"It's a jolly walk round the lake," he said, "but tonight I think we'll take the steamer. It's about a quarter of a mile nearer from the Briesau [Perti-sau] landing stage than it is from here."

The little steamer waited ten minutes, then her whistle blew and off she went – first to Buchau at

the opposite side of the lake, and then to Briesau
. . . From the landing-stage to the Chalet was a
good ten minutes' walk, and then they saw the
welcoming lights. They were at the Chalet School
at last. (*The School at the Chalet*)

For the present-day traveller to Pertisau much in
Elinor's descriptions will still seem familiar – the
grassy meadows on the alm, the Tirolean farmhouses
and chalets with dark wooden exteriors highlighted
by window-boxes of exuberantly coloured flowers,
the wonderful views over the lake and mountains,
and the genuine friendliness of the local people. It is
even possible to find Elinor's famous plumeaus on
the beds!

Pertisau today remains an appealing place. There
have obviously been changes since Elinor's early
books, and in July and August the lakeside is likely
to resemble, in the words of one disappointed Chalet
fan, "Blackpool on Bank Holiday". But, even in
high season, peace and solitude can still be found by
striking inland and taking the more remote mountain
paths. In the village itself, the old Fürstenhaus
Hotel, the original of the "Kron Prinz Karl", has
been rebuilt, and the "little whitewashed chapel" of
the stories no longer stands behind it. But many
local features that are familiar to readers can still be
seen: the landing-stages used by the steamers,
exactly where they should be, "just past the Kron
Prinz Karl"; the Post Hotel, the way down through
the pine woods to Jenbach/Spärtz; the broad easy
path up to the Bärenbad Alm; the high narrow cliff

37

path, past the "Dripping Rock", to Gaisalm. And nothing can alter the extraordinary beauty of the lake and mountains.

Looking round the terrain, it is clear what it was that suggested to Elinor some of the incidents in her stories. Thick mists and hailstorms can descend on the mountains without a moment's warning, and it is frighteningly easy to get lost on the steep and thickly wooded slopes, where there may be a precipice just round the corner. The wisest course is to take a detailed map, and to stick to the marked paths. But of course, had the Chalet girls done this, many of their exciting adventures would never have taken place!

To pinpoint the School's probable location is not difficult, for the descriptions in the early books are so detailed and – for Elinor – so unusually consistent, that it is possible to make a list of precise conditions. The site has to be near, though not immediately on the lakeside; it has to be in a position that commands views of the lake in one direction and, in the other, of the mountains behind Pertisau. It has to be on, slightly higher ground than the waterfront, and at a fair distance from the "Kron Priz Karl"; and, if it is to fit the description "a good ten minutes' walk" from the steamers' landing-stages, it has to be situated well towards the Seespitz end of the village. To narrow the field still more, it has to be further south along the lakeside than the Post Hotel, since in order to reach the Post it was necessary to turn left from the Chalet. Finally, there has to be a garden round it – something quite unusual in Pertisau.

Taking these factors into account, one site does fulfil all the required conditions: that of the Alpenhof Hotel, formerly one of the leading hotels in Pertisau though now empty and sadly dilapidated. Not that the hotel itself can ever have looked much like the descriptions of the Chalet School. But in imagination it can easily be replaced with one of the more traditional chalets Elinor describes:

"The building was [made] of wood and plaster, like most of the buildings in the Tiern Valley . . . A fresco . . . adorned the walls . . . [and a] balcony . . . ran all round the house . . . about ten feet above the ground . . . [At the windows were] window boxes full of geraniums and marguerites."

Naturally it is not possible to identify all the places in the stories. Some are obviously imaginary. These include "Mechthau", the little village the exhausted girls reach after their long climb up the mountain from Gaisalm (*Rivals of the Chalet School*); the "Valley of the Flowers" (*Exploits of the Chalet Girls* and *New House at the Chalet School*); the Robin's cave, hidden among the crags near the Sonnalpe (*The Chalet School in Exile*) and the Bäumersee, near which the Chalet Guides pitch their camp and have many adventures (*Chalet Girls in Camp*). Regarding the latter, many readers are convinced that this delightful lake does exist, but although the Ordnance Survey reveals numerous small, unnamed lakes in the mountainous regions above the Achensee, none of them quite fits the description of the Bäumersee.

There are of course a large number of real places

which appear in the stories under their proper names and in their correct locations. Among these are Innsbruck, Hall, Eben, Maurach, Seespitz, Buchau, Seehof, Scholastika, Gaisalm (with the "Dripping Rock"), the Bärenbad and Bärenkopf mountains, and the Post Hotel. There is also a handful of places which appear in their correct locations but under made-up names – Pertisau being changed to Briesau, Achensee to Tiernsee, Jenbach to Spärtz, Achenkirch to Tiernkirch, and Fürstenhaus to Kron Prinz Karl.

Finally there is a group of places, all of them important in the stories, which combine real life and Elinor's imagination. To complicate things further, these places may have real, or made-up, or even "transferred" names. Take the "Tiern Valley": in fiction this leads from the head of the village of Briesau through the mountains, passing the small hamlet of "Lauterbach", and eventually crossing by way of the "Tiern Pass" into Germany. It is thus a semi-fiction amalgam of the three different valleys which, in real life, wander off into the mountains behind Pertisau. None of these three, however, is headed by a pass into Germany, although the real-life Achen Pass, at the north end of the lake, does lead across the frontier into Bavaria.

Then there is the little village of "Torteswald", where the Maranis and Gertrud Steinbrücke are living in the early chapters of *The School at the Chalet*. "Torteswald" is said to be "twenty minutes' walk from Seespitz", so must lie between the real-life Maurach and Eben. And here Elinor's choice of

40

the particular pseudonym is interesting, for it must surely have been suggested to her by the name Torteval, a real place in Guernsey which she had visited the summer before her Tirolean holiday.

Another of Elinor's favoured names is "Lauterbach" (mentioned above). In the Tirolean books it is given to the small hamlet, two or three miles up the Tiern valley, which has a real-life parallel in the cluster of chalets and farm buildings at the head of the Falzthurntal. Later, in the Swiss books, Elinor uses the name again, this time as a pseudonym for Lauterbrunnen near Interlaken.

But far more important than either Torteswald or Lauterbach is the Sonnalpe, which plays a major role in the stories from the second book onwards. It is here, on a mountain shelf high above the Tiernsee, that Doctor Russell establishes the Sanatorium which will always be closely associated with the Chalet School. And it is here that he builds Die Rosen, the pretty chalet where he and Madge live after their marriage and where David and Sybil, their first two children, are born. The Sonnalpe is described as being "on the opposite side of the Tiernsee" from the Chalet School; and there is, in fact, among the rocky peaks above Buchau and Maurach – thus in the correct area – a mountain shelf named the Sonnwendhübel; there is even an alm with a few huts. No sanatorium, though!

Almost as important as the Sonnalpe is the "Tiernjoch" mountain. This is said to be the giant of all the mountains round the Tiernsee; and at first glance it seems the real-life Sonnjoch would be the nearest equivalent, since it is the highest mountain near Portisau and its situation in the Falzthurn valley also fits the stories quite well. However, the hazardous ascent of the "Tiernjoch" so vividly depicted in *The School at the Chalet* does not match the real ascent of the Sonnjoch, for this, although a long haul, is not considered a dangerous climb. On the other hand, the real-life Mondscheinspitze, which the local guidebooks place in the category "only for the very experienced mountaineer", sounds remarkably like Elinor's "Tiernjoch". That "worst bit of all", for example:

Here, for one hundred and fifty yards, the path, barely three feet wide in most places, and even less in some, crawled along the edge of a precipice which went sheer down to the valley far below. On the other side, a wall of stark rock arose, also sheerly, giving no hold of any kind. This was the place where anyone in the least degree nervous was always roped, and it was where the worst accidents always occurred.

And that is exactly what happens on the climb up the Mondscheinspitze – the real one, that is; for, to confuse matters further, Elinor has bestowed the name "Mondscheinspitze" on quite a different mountain:

The climb up the Mondscheinspitze is remarkably easy. There is a well-defined path, which winds in and out among the dark trees, every now and then coming out into narrow – very narrow – grassy ledges. Presently, however, it left the woods, and . . . climbed up the bare limestone face of the mountain beneath the glare of the July sun. Tufts of grass, with wild scabious and white marguerites, punctuated the way, and gorgeous butterflies fluttered round . . . so little afraid that often they settled on hat or frock.

Plainly this cannot be the *real* Mondscheinspitze. The mountain that comes nearest to the above description is probably one called the Feilkopf, which stands near the opening of the Pletzach valley – the farthest north of the three valleys behind Pertisau. The ascent here could fairly be described, in the words of Frieda Mensch's father, as "a nice little climb"; and from the summit the view corresponds with that seen by the Chalet girls from the top of *their* Mondscheinspitze:

At their feet lay the valley they had crossed that morning, cool and green, with the empty river bed stretching like a white ribbon down its length. In the distance they could see Briesau, lying like a toy village some giant child had set out; and beyond it . . . the Tiern See, a living sapphire, gleamed beneath the sun.

So was that the Mondscheinspitze or the Feilkopf? In the end it hardly matters: the girls of the Chalet School inhabit a landscape which owes as much to Elinor as to the real world.

43

Part Two – *The Chalet School on the Move*

The Chalet School's happy years in Tirol came to a dramatic end with the Nazi annexation of Austria. For a brief interval the school then took refuge in an empty hotel on the Sonnalpe, named Der Edel Ritter (*The Chalet School in Exile*); and the Sonnalpe, as already discussed, belongs to the category of places which mingle real life and imagination – in other words, places that are set in a real life background but either do not exist at all, or, if they do exist, have been renamed. Once the stories move from the Tiernsee it is not possible to state with the same assurance exactly where the school is situated, because that first Tirolean setting differs from all the subsequent locations in some important respects. First, "Briesau" is a real place, pictured for the most part exactly as it is in real life. And once identified as Pertisau, it can be visited. There are even maps available in Britain showing the layout of the village. The Tirolean books (and there are fourteen of them) also contain a wealth of detail about the scenery and topography of the district, with real names being used in many cases. But the most important point of difference is that Elinor did personally confirm that Pertisau was the place she'd had in mind; and this she never did regarding any of the school's later locations – quite possibly finding that being tied to a real place was too limiting.

For example, the house known as "Sarres", which becomes the Chalet School's temporary home in Guernsey and their first stop after leaving the Tirol, is never placed exactly. Minute details are available about the colour-wash on the walls, the paintwork in deep soft green, the plain net curtains "that had come from Tyrol", and the gleamingly polished floors. The garden, restored after "years of neglect", is also described. But at no point can the reader learn the exact situation of "Sarres"; only that the house – as Madge informs Joey – is "not far from Jerbourg, where they intend to have the Sanatorium". That gives some indication, for the Jerbourg peninsula in Guernsey is a real place; it forms the extreme south-east corner of the island and there are wonderful views from the cliff paths around its jagged coastline. Jerbourg, lying as it does relatively high above the sea, certainly benefits from plenty of fresh breezes, and it would probably have been as good a place as any for the Sanatorium and school. However, the time spent in Guernsey is so short that Elinor has little opportunity to fill in the background to any great extent. (Her "La Rochelle" books, on the other hand, show a considerable feeling for the atmosphere and scenery of the Channel Islands.)

Various Guernsey places are mentioned in *The Chalet School in Exile* which do exist. The Russells, for example, live at Torteval, and the Maynards "not far from St Pierre du Bois". The Chalet girls go on an expedition to Pleinmont – where, so one of them declares, "the Gens de Vendredi keep Witches' Sabbath every Friday night" – and on the way they pass "the great sweep of Rocquaine Bay", and the little cottage, "La Rochelle", which belongs now to the Lucy family. but the precise location of the Chalet School is never made clear.

Nor is it a simple matter, when the school moves on to "Armishire", to state exactly where "Plas Howell", their new home, is situated. Various interesting suggestions have been made by readers, who have also pinpointed certain sites as the possible originals of Joey's home, "Plas Gwyn", and the "Round House" where Madge's family lived. But Elinor herself never revealed whether she had been thinking of real places.

However, there are five books covering this period, which contain many descriptive details; and of course both "Armiford" and "Armishire" are real places, being pseudonyms for Hereford, and the county then known as Herefordshire – now Hereford and Worcester. What is more, Elinor was herself living in Hereford at the time she wrote these books, and plainly she drew on her own experience in describing the locality, just as she did in the Tirolean

46

books. Hence a knowledge of her day-to-day life during this period, helped by some acquaintance with the district, can provide numerous clues to the school's putative whereabouts.

First of all, "Howell Village", the nearest place to Plas Howell: the stories make clear that this village lies in the attractively named Golden Valley, about fourteen miles from Armiford/Hereford. In other words, in exactly the same district, towards the Black Mountains and "on the English side of the Welsh border", is the real-life village of Peterchurch, a place Elinor had visited regularly in term-time during the four and a half years she worked as a daily governess. Not being a driver, she had always travelled by bus, and there is undoubtedly a remarkable likeness between the real-life journey from Peterchurch to Hereford and the one so often described in the stories from "Howell" to "Armiford".

Consider for a moment two passages from *Highland Twins at the Chalet School*. In both, the details are exactly true to real life, apart from a few alterations to street and place names.

In the first, Joey Maynard has left her home in the Golden Valley at a very early hour, and is driving in to Armiford station. A few miles after leaving Plas Gwyn she "changed gears for the steep hill, driving carefully for the road was not wide . . .

Halfway to Armiford, she passed the new, big aerodrome where already a large village of houses had grown up . . . Once past this place . . . she pushed ahead, for before long she would turn on

47

to the main road between Armiford and the nearest county town [i.e. Monmouth], and she knew well that . . . she would find it packed with lorries . . . It was just twenty past six when she entered the built-up area of Armiford [and drove] down the long road with its houses on either side which began below the railway bridge. She made the sharp turn where the Sors road [Sors being an anagram of Ross, i.e. Ross-on-Wye] runs into what is known as Fairmount [Belmont] Road, crossed the old stone bridge . . . and turned into King Street, and thence through Broad Street, past the cathedral . . . and then through the bottleneck of High Street and across the fine quadrangle of High Town where most of the best shops in Armiford stand. Past the Old House . . . and so down narrow St Stephen's Gate [really St Peter's Street] into the magnificent sweep of Broome Road [Commercial Road] past the big chapel and bus station at one side [both are still there, just as described], and then up the station approach, till she drew up at one side of the station.

More precise directions to the station in *Hereford* would be hard to find!

The second passage, which occurs only a few pages later, concentrates more on the countryside end of the return journey.

First,

. . . through the now busy streets of Armiford. Then . . . under a railway bridge . . . and into a country road with fields and hedges on both sides, and, in the distance, the long gentle slopes of the Black Mountains. Jo pointed them out, explaining that some of them were more difficult [to climb] than they looked . . . then swung the car round a sharp corner, past the aerodrome, and so up the slope of a steep hill. [From] the top . . . they coasted down another slope, with the land rising on either side.

Probably the most striking feature of these two passages is the almost obsessive accuracy they show. And similar accounts are given in several other books. Some are more detailed than others, but nearly all mention certain features of this journey which do exist in real life. That railway bridge, for one – it appears in both the passages quoted, and it still exists, although the line is no longer in use. Also, the "sharp corner" near the aerodrome, which is still there too, although oddly enough it is not shown on ordinary maps. And the steep hill, frequently mentioned in other books, is probably that known locally as the "Batcho Hill".

The seven "Armishire" books do establish conclusively that "Plas Howell" lay somewhere in the neighbourhood of Peterchurch, or Vowchurch, or one of the nearby villages in the Golden Valley. There are even clues suggesting that Elinor may have had a specific site in mind. But the secret of its exact position was not one she ever shared in real life.

On the other hand, she was lavish with details about Plas Howell itself, and poured out long affectionate descriptions in most of the Armishire books. A good introduction to the house is to see it through the eyes of a new girl, Jacynth Hardy, who comes from "the industrial north" just as Elinor did. Jacynth is travelling in the school bus from Armiford to Plas Howell and, at first, the journey closely resembles the second of the passages quoted above. Then . . .

. . . . at last they reached a broad drive with high wooden gates set open and a pretty lodge at one side. Up this they went and [past] wide green spaces with tall copper beeches, clumps of elms and stately lombardy poplars. Here and there, may bushes filled the air with a delicious almond scent, and at one point masses of rhododendrons gleamed with buds as yet unfurled. Then [through] a second gate, and [into] the garden proper. A great stretch of green lawn swept up to the house, and tennis courts were netted off at its foot. Nearer to the house were flower beds filled with standard roses [and] wallflowers, in blood-red, gold, and mahogany gowns, added their sweetness to the air. And above all rose the great house, once white, but now weathered to gracious tones of grey. [It] stood on an embankment, and a broad stone terrace ran round it, fenced off from the grassy banks . . . by a palisading of low stone pillars. Leading up to the great front door were semi-circular steps, and tall, classical pillars with beautifully carved capitals.

And anyone who would like to see inside this imposing house can follow another new girl, the ten-year-old Mary-Lou Trelawney. A few years after Jacynth, she is escorted up the semi-circular steps and through the great front door, to make her first entrance into the Chalet School where she will later become such an influential person.

Mrs Maynard . . . led them into a spacious hall which had statues here and there, and plants and bowls of flowers set on the tables and window-sill. There were several old chairs of heavy oak, and an oak settle, nearly black with age, stood beside the wide fireplace . . . The morning sun streamed through the big stained-glass window on the landing above [the hall], and cast reflections of crimson, blue and yellow on the polished floor. A beautiful oak staircase ran up to it, and then turned and went on to an upper corridor.

Plas Howell obviously merits the description "a great mansion", which is often bestowed on it. In fact it sounds rather on the grand side to make really comfortable premises for a school, even one so relatively well behaved as the Chalet School. One can understand Miss Annersley's reaction on her first visit there when she sees "the noble room with its built-in shelves laden with books, its comfortable saddle-bag chairs and sofa, its Chinese carpet in glowing blues and oranges" which is to be the official headmistress's study, and asks doubtfully: "Are you sure this is the room Mr Howell meant, Jo?" Nor was this the first shock the Head has received that day. Earlier on her tour of the house she had "uttered an exclamation of dismay" on seeing that the drawing-room walls were covered with an expensive-looking French wallpaper in satin stripes; and since this elegant drawing room was to be the school assembly hall, Miss Annersley's dismay is not surprising.

However, all round, Plas Howell had much to recommend it, and it is only when "trouble with the drains" is diagnosed that the Chalet School, after about eight happy years, is forced to move elsewhere.

The next setting, for the first time in the series, *is* entirely imaginary. There is a real place called St Briavels, but this lies between Monmouth and Chepstow, not far from Tintern, and it is definitely not an island. The stories give various descriptions of the fictional St Briavels, and two in particular are interesting because they appear to contradict each other. One states it to be "an island – in the Irish Sea off Wales"; the other "an island off the coast of South Wales" (the Irish Sea lying, of course, off the west coast of Wales). But since St Briavels makes no claim to be a real place, the discrepancy could be viewed as part of its mythological status.

The island setting gives the school plenty of scope for new activities – rowing and bird-watching and so on – as well as for continuing with established pastimes like gardening and tennis. And Elinor is able to use the natural hazards of island life, among them tides, mists, and rock scrambling, to provide a number of exciting adventures.

As regards the house on St Briavels, this was known simply as the Big House. It is not described as extensively as was Plas Howell, but appears to have been especially well endowed with windows: at one side of "the deeply recessed front door [there were] three wide bow windows"; on the other, "three sets of French windows"; and above them, "two rows of flat Georgian windows with small panes". And the spacious grounds include not only lawns, flower borders and shrubberies, but a couple of tennis courts and an orchard. Once again the Chalet School had fallen on its feet.

In passing, the village of "Carnbach" should be mentioned; it is from Carnbach, on the Welsh mainland opposite St Briavels, that the ferry sails to the island. It is at Carnbach that a house is found for the branch of the school that remains in Britain; and the house, "Cartref", where Joey and her family spend about a year, is on the outskirts of Carnbach.

For seven terms the Chalet School remains in St Briavels. Then, some two and a half years after their arrival on the island, the final move takes place, this time to the Bernese Oberland.

Part Three – *The Swiss Years*

For most pupils of the Chalet School, the adventure in Switzerland begins only in the thirtieth book, *The Chalet School and Barbara*. But an advance party had already launched into the Oberland a year earlier. Then (as narrated in *The Chalet School in the Oberland*) a group of older girls, including a fair number from other schools, had travelled to "Welsen" to join the finishing or post-sixth-form branch that was being opened there under the headship of Miss Wilson.

The places named in the Swiss books are, like those in Tirol and Armishire, a mixture of the real and the imaginary. Basle, Zurich, Lucerne, Geneva, Montreux, and Berne, for example, all figure in the stories at different points, and receive descriptions, often in some detail. But we are never told more than the approximate location of either Welsen or the Görnetz Platz, which from this point onwards is home to the Maynard family as well as to the Chalet School and the Sanatorium.

A few clues are scattered around, however. Miss Annersley mentions the complicated journey to the Oberland:

"By train from London. We cross the Channel by the train ferry and so to Paris. We change at Paris to a train for Berne, and in Berne we change again for Interlaken, which will be our nearest town of any size. From there, we take the mountain train up to the Platz."

She appears to have forgotten that yet another change would be required in Interlaken. Here, as many of the books do mention, it is necessary to transfer, on foot or otherwise, from the West Station to the East, (Interlaken Ost Bahnhof being the starting point for the mountain railway, both in the stories and in real life). And it is possible to guess the approximate location of Welsen from the account of another journey.

"Here we are!" Miss Norton suddenly exclaimed, as the little train came to a stop at a long, rather narrow alp. "Pick up your belongings, girls, and hurry along! The train won't wait all day!"

The girls tumbled out hurriedly . . . then the row of small carriages moved off and they were left standing, sniffing the fresh sweet air that came to them from the great mountains.

The Bahnhof, so-called, at Lauterbach consisted of a kind of sideless shed on either side of the line. At the gate at one end stood a man in a loose blue blouse and peaked cap, ready to take the tickets.

The only clue here (the ticket collector and the sideless shed could be anywhere) is the name "Lauterbach". It was, of course, the pseudonym Elinor had used in the Tirolean books for a hamlet at the head of the Tiern Valley. But in this context, and remembering the proximity of Interlaken, it is clear that Lauterbach must be a disguise for the real Lauterbrunnen. And so the possible location of Welsen begins to emerge.

The way from Lauterbach/Lauterbrunnen to the new school premises at Welsen is

. . . a pleasant walk, up a twisting path worn in the limestone of the mountain. Bushes grew on either side . . . late-blooming flowers [and] here and there . . . clumps of stone pines . . . It took . . . about twenty minutes to climb up, but at last they reached the top and found themselves standing on rough pasture, dotted here and there with chalets, some little more than huts, others larger. Straight ahead of them was a big one set in a garden where roses still bloomed bravely.

This was Das Haus unter den Kiefern (the House under the Pines) where the new branch of the school was to settle. The fact that it could be reached in about twenty minutes' walking time from Lauterbach/Lauterbrunnen gives some idea of Welsen's imagined position. This is further clarified in a later chapter, when the school party makes an expedition on foot to the "Wengeralp" – plainly an adaptation of the real life Wengenalp – thus placing Welsen as definitely on the east, or Wengen, side of the Lauterbrunnen valley.

This helps with the identification of the Görnetz Platz – or at least of its situation. The "Görnetz Platz" as such does not exist, but various details given in the stories suggest that "Görnetz Village" is a kind of amalgam of two real-life villages, those of Wengen and Mürren. As Miss Burnett, the Chalet School's teacher of PE, explains while the school bus is carefully making its way up the spectacular road to the Görnetz Platz:

"There are at least thirty or forty chalets dotted about the Platz, including a couple of shops, one of which is the post office . . . and there are two churches – a Protestant one and a Catholic chapel which is served from an Augustinian convent a few miles away."

This, in size and layout, fits better with Mürren than with Wengen, which is considerably the larger place – over thirteen hundred inhabitants to Mürren's four hundred and fifty odd. On the other hand, Mürren, being to the west and south of Lauterbrunnen, is on the wrong side of the valley to meet the often repeated description "in the mountains above Welsen", since the latter was definitely on the east of Lauterbrunnen.

57

However, there is little point in trying too hard to identify a place which is, after all, imaginary. Elinor undoubtedly had more freedom this way, and probably found description considerably easier if nothing had to fit precisely with a real place.

JOEY'S FAMILY

Just like a Charlotte Yonge family! – people in the Chalet School books often make this comment about the Maynards. And although today the comparison may not convey much to some readers, anyone familiar with the once-popular Victorian novelist, Charlotte Mary Yonge, will know exactly what to expect. The families in books by Miss Yonge seem always to include at least nine or ten children; quite frequently there are more, with pairs of twins being a common occurrence. Elinor is known to have admired Charlotte Yonge, and certainly her own stories include a striking number of large families, Joey's being of course the most numerous of all.

The odd thing is, so far as Joey is concerned, that she in her schooldays had frequently been heard proclaiming that marriage and children were not for her. No indeed! Her friends might all get married if they wished. She would always remain single. For she was going to be the delightful maiden aunt that every family needed. And plainly there would have

FAMILY TREE

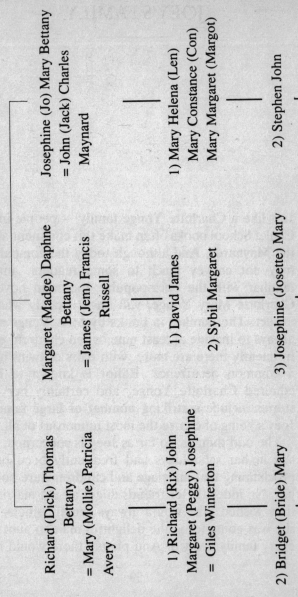

Richard (Dick) Thomas Bettany
= Mary (Mollie) Patricia Avery

Margaret (Madge) Daphne Bettany
= James (Jem) Francis Russell

Josephine (Jo) Mary Bettany
= John (Jack) Charles Maynard

1) Richard (Rix) John
Margaret (Peggy) Josephine
= Giles Winterton

2) Bridget (Bride) Mary

1) David James

2) Sybil Margaret

3) Josephine (Josette) Mary

1) Mary Helena (Len)
Mary Constance (Con)
Mary Margaret (Margot)

2) Stephen John

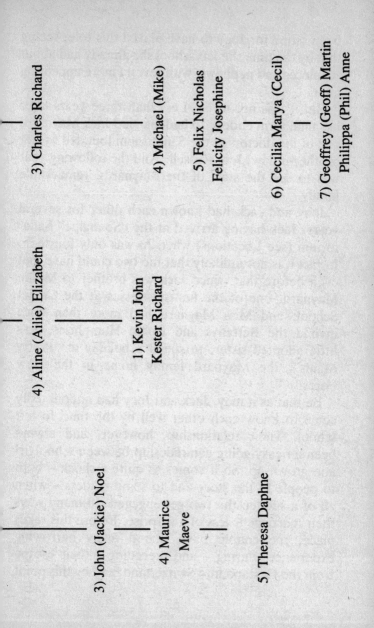

3) Charles Richard

4) Michael (Mike)

5) Felix Nicholas
Felicity Josephine

6) Cecilia Marya (Cecil)

7) Geoffrey (Geoff) Martin
Philippa (Phil) Anne

4) Aline (Ailie) Elizabeth

1) Kevin John
Kester Richard

3) John (Jackie) Noel

4) Maurice
Maeve

5) Theresa Daphne

been scope for Joey to have played this role, seeing that by the time she left school she already had about six nieces and nephews, with several more appearing later.

But it was not to be. Less than three years after her final term ended, Jo had married Jack Maynard, one of the doctors at the Sanatorium founded by her brother-in-law, Jem Russell. And the following year was to see the start of the Maynards' remarkable family.

Joey and Jack had known each other for several years, Jack having arrived at the "Sonnalpe" Sanatorium (see Locations) when Jo was only fourteen. In fact it is not unlikely that the two could have met even before that, since Jack was brother to Mollie Maynard, one of the first mistresses at the Chalet School; and Miss Maynard had more than once invited the Bettanys and Robin Humphries, Jo's little adopted sister, to spend a holiday at "Pretty Maids", the Maynard family home in the New Forest.

Be that as it may, Jack and Joey had undoubtedly come to know each other well by the time Jo left school. Their relationship, however, had always been an easy-going comradeship between schoolgirl and grown-up. So it comes as quite a shock – both to people in the story and to some readers – when all of a sudden the two get engaged. In many ways their marriage is less of a surprise. Before this takes place, the couple have shared many harrowing experiences during – and preceding – their escape from the Gestapo into Switzerland; and by this point enough time has passed for everyone to grow used to the idea.

Anyway, marriage is not allowed to quench Jo's unfailingly effervescent spirits, and she continues to do things "differently". Everyone expects this, of course. So it seems well in character when her family begins with not just one baby, or even twins, but with triplets. (And, on another level, that immediately put Elinor Brent-Dyer well ahead in the school-story stakes: the grown-up heroines in other series had been quite in the habit of producing twins – one actually manages two pairs in less than a year – but no-one before had ever achieved triplets.)

From the start Joey's three daughters are different in character though they at least begin by looking alike. In particular, all three have red hair – this to the vast amusement of Jo's elder sister, for Madge recalls that when *her* daughter Sybil arrived, some years earlier, Jo had made unflattering comments about the baby's "ginger" hair. And at first the triplets, like all new babies, have blue eyes. Later the colours begin to change, becoming, eventually, in one case grey, in another dark brown, and only in one remaining blue.

And Joey, not content with merely having triplets, has still a few more bombshells to explode. To begin with she outrages her sister by referring to the three babies, with a perfectly straight face, as One, Two and Three – ("'Give me Three . . . and you can put Two back into the cradle . . .'"). Madge comments, that she "'. . . might have known Jo wouldn't be sensible, even over her children'". Nor is she better pleased when Jo suggests next that the triplets are to be called Jane, Joan, and Jean. Madge has to wait two days before she – and incidentally the reader – can learn that Jack and Joey have really decided to give each child Mary as a first name; then the eldest is to be Helena, after the Chalet School's very own Miss Wilson; the second Constance, after Miss Stewart, teacher of history in the Chalet School since Jo's own early days there; and the third Margaret, after Madge herself. The approved shortenings for these names have also been chosen. Margaret is to be known as Margot (this, partly as a gesture in memory of Jem Russell's late sister, Margot Venables); Constance will be shortened to Connie – in fact it very soon becomes Con; and Helena is to be Len. The latter choice has a personal connection with Elinor, who used this particular abbreviation of her own name for many years; one friend who first knew Elinor in the 1920s still refers to her as "Len".

In the end, no great surprises about those names. But the announcement that Joey and Jack's children will call their parents "Mamma" and "Papa" does cause a fair amount of stir.

"Oh, I'm not going to be *Mummy* to them," said Jo, comfortably assured that she was going to make a small sensation by her next statement.

"What, then? [enquires Violet Allison, a member of the Chalet School's Sixth Form]. Small children find *Mother* awfully difficult to say. You surely aren't going all modern and letting them call you *Jo*?"

"No fear! Jack would have something to say about *that*. He has quite old-fashioned ideas in some ways, you know. No; they're going to call me Mamma, and him Papa." And Joey grinned as she saw Violet's jaw drop.

"Mamma and Papa! Joey! What on earth *for*? I thought no one ever did in these days."

"Then I'll set the fashion."

And for several years Jack and Joey are indeed to be addressed by their children as Papa and Mamma; although later they do have to compromise a little with contemporary ideas, and in due course the Maynards make use of Daddy, Mother, and various other forms of address. Jo, however, steadfastly refuses to answer to "Ma"!

The three little girls, Len, Con, and Margot, spend the first months of their lives at "Les Rosiers", the villa in Guernsey where Joey and Jack had settled down soon after their arrival from Switzerland. Few details are available about this, Joey's first married home, apart from the fact that the house was in the parish of Le Forêt, although apparently not far from St Pierre du Bois. (Today, Joey might be less ready to choose this district, since the Guernsey airport is situated at Le Forêt.) In any case the Maynards have only a short time at "Les Rosiers", for soon wartime conditions make it imperative for Jo and her family to leave Guernsey. First they endure a hair-raising journey across the channel; then find their way by stages to "Armishire" where, conveniently, a house has fallen vacant in "Howell Village" (see Locations).

This house, "Plas Gwyn" is described in several books: "It was a very pretty house . . . with white walls, in accordance with its name . . . and roses and honeysuckle climbing up [them]. [There was a] big French window on the left of the porch [and] inside the house . . . an impression of coolness and peace . . . and the scent of flowers."

"Plas Gwyn" is to be the Maynards' home for seven or more years, and to see the birth of three boys – not triplets this time but, as Joey often calls it, "singletons". The boys are named Stephen, Charles Richard, and Michael. (The name Charles is said to be Joey's favourite among boys' names, but interestingly it was also the name of Elinor Brent-Dyer's own father.)

By the time another move looms up, the triplets are eight and a half, Stephen six, Charles four and three-quarters, and Michael almost a year old. The boys, both in appearance and in character, are a mixed bunch. Stephen is fair-haired, sturdy, steady and dependable; Charles has black hair and very dark grey eyes; he tends to be delicate, but is in a quiet way an influential person in the family despite his tender years. Michael, almost always known as Mike, has fair curly hair and blue eyes; at times he can look like a baby angel but he is by far the naughtiest of the three.

The triplets also vary in temperament and colouring, although all three still have a strong family resemblance. Len's thick wavy hair has deepened from the original red to chestnut brown, and her eyes are now smoky grey – Elinor sometimes likens

66

their colour to wood violets. Con has become as dark in hair and eyes as Joey herself; while Margot's short curly hair is reddish gold and her eyes a brilliant blue. Of the three, Len is the natural leader and the most generous in nature; Con is a dreamer, and has inherited some of her mother's story-telling gifts; Margot is the family rebel, with a quick wit and a tendency to be sharp-tongued. She is also the member of the family whose health most often gives her parents cause for anxiety, for she is especially prone to bronchitis. And because Jack and Joey feel that a winter away from Britain would benefit Margot's health they agree, with the greatest reluctance on Joey's part, to let the child go to Canada for some months with Madge and Jem Russell. This separation eventually extends for a year; and in the meantime the Maynard family are compelled once again to look for another house, though in this case only a temporary one. As Miss Annersley explains to Peggy Bettany: "'. . . your aunt is leaving Plas Gwyn for the present . . . No; it isn't drains like Plas Howell. It's something almost as alarming though. Part of the foundations has begun to subside, and the house isn't safe.'"

Luckily, a friend offers Jo the use of "Cartref", a house near "Carnbach" – the village on the Welsh mainland just opposite "St Briavels" (see Locations), and Jo is thus able to maintain regular contact with the school.

"It's a lot smaller than Plas Gwyn" [Peggy Bettany remarks on her first visit to Cartref].

"How right you are! . . . Still we were lucky to get anywhere . . . We'll just have to put up with being a bit cramped for the next few months. It'll make us appreciate Plas Gwyn when we go back," Jo said philosophically.

Of course the family numbers are reduced for the time being, with Margot absent in Canada. And the Maynards' sojourn at "Cartref" does not last very long. The following spring, about six months later, the whole family is off to Canada, where Jack has "to attend an important medical conference". Here, in Toronto, Len and Con are at last reunited with their third triplet, who has grown several inches and is dramatically improved in health.

Joey, her husband, and their six children are to remain in Toronto throughout the next year; and during their stay the Maynard family is increased to eight by the arrival of twins – Felix Nicholas and Felicity Josephine – who are both silvery fair in colouring. In the meantime Len and Con have joined Margot at La Sagesse Convent School, where they soon learn "to chatter French like natives"; and parents and children alike flourish in the "crisp dry cold" of the Canadian winter.

Next, it's back again to "Plas Gwyn". But not for long this time: when the Maynards arrive in Britain they find the Chalet School already in the midst of preparing to follow the Sanatorium to Switzerland. And since Jack Maynard has now been appointed head of the San, this means that Joey and her flock must face a mass removal almost at once.

For Jo, the pangs of parting from "Plas Gwyn", her beloved house in the Golden Valley, are tempered by the joyful prospect of returning to live in the Alps. And her new home on the "Görnetz Platz" (see Locations) certainly has much to offer.

Jo stopped short in the middle of the broad pathway and stood gazing. She saw a very big, four-storied house with plastered walls, frescoed and banded with three balconies reaching from the ground floor to the third floor. The wooden posts were carved and the close-set railings were high enough to prevent any accidents with heedless youngsters. The deep-pitched roof was weighted with heavy stones, roped on in the usual fashion of the Alps, and there were four dormer windows set in it. Beneath came six small ones of the lattice type. The main bedroom floor had French windows opening on to the balcony, and on the ground floor there were three windows on each side of the door. The house stood on a little eminence and the front door was reached by half a dozen steps built sideways to the house.

[Inside] Jo found herself in a square hall with a door opening on either hand and a passage running across the back.

"*This* isn't a proper chalet," she said.

"As I keep telling you, it was a *pension*," her husband said, exaggerated patience in his tones. "It was built for that purpose – and very well built, too, I may add. This room on the right used to be the Speisesaal; and as it has a hatch through

69

to the kitchen, I vote we keep it [as the dining-room]."

"I couldn't agree more. Then which [is] the Saal? [drawing-room]."

But Jack tells her she must decide for herself about that. And the moment Joey has entered a long spacious room at the back of the house, she does not hesitate: "Oh Jack! There's no question, of course! This is the one . . . How could you ask when it has that view of the Jungfrau?"

And so the huge elegant room, that had been the ballroom of the former "Pension Wellington", becomes the heart of the Maynard family's new home. And a name is chosen to signify the role this house is destined to play in the lives of many, even beyond their family circle: "Freudesheim" – "Happy Home".

One old friend who receives a specially warm welcome at "Freudesheim" is Grizel Cochrane – that same Grizel who was among the Chalet School's very first pupils. Grizel has been living in New Zealand for many years, and she has never met the latest additions to the Maynard household.

As she sits enjoying an "English tea" with Joey, a "clatter of small feet . . . and the thud of paddy-paws" herald an eruption into the drawing-room. Bounding ahead comes a huge golden and white St Bernard.

Just for one instant Grizel's thoughts go to Rufus – the beloved St Bernard who, as a puppy, was rescued from drowning by the youthful Joey, to become thereafter her faithful companion all through her schooldays and onwards. "'Joey! This isn't – but of course it isn't! I remember dear old Rufus dying when you were at Cartref. Is this a son of his?'

'No; Bruno was a gift from the school the second term we were up here. I'd been talking of having another dog, but I couldn't make up my mind to doing it. Then the girls gave me Bruno and he has his own place – though never Rufus's.'"

Next Grizel is introduced to the ninth, tenth and eleventh of Joey's family, all born since the Maynards arrived in Switzerland. First, five-year-old Cecil – short for Cecilia Marya, the real name of Jo's adopted sister Robin Humphries, who is Cecil's godmother. Then the twins, Philippa and Geoffrey, who "will be two in June". Phil and Geoff, as they are known, are both red-headed, but Cecil has dark curly hair and black eyes.

"'You always said you meant to have the longest family of all . . .' [Grizel remarks later]. 'Eleven, isn't it? I hope you're satisfied.'

'. . . Oh, you never know . . . [I might] think of quads as a nice round off.'"

But even Grizel, who has never had much sense of humour, doesn't take this threat too seriously.

Phil and Geoff are in fact to be the last additions to the Maynard family. (Would they have remained the last, had Elinor lived to add more books to the series . . . ? Who can tell?)

Joey was of course lucky in always having excellent domestic help. As a result she seems to be

71

spared much of the nitty-gritty of housework. True, she is often pictured in the throes of looking after her numerous children; she can sometimes be seen in the kitchen or immersed in a sea of mending; she has to cope with a vast number of illnesses and childish ailments – not to mention the horrendous bouts of teething trouble which seem to afflict most of her babies; but she never apparently has much truck with sweeping and dusting – although it must have needed a deal of hard work, even in the clean air of mountain Switzerland, to keep that enormous house spick and span, as it always was. But neither did Jo have to spend hours shopping in order to replenish the family's larder. No doubt all these matters were taken care of by the faithful Anna and the co-adjutor – as Anna's assistant was always known.

It helped, too, that Joey's children were all brought up, very sensibly, to be helpful around the house from an early age. And anyway it was only during holidays that everyone was at home. Before the end of the series the Maynard girls have all become pupils at the Chalet School – with the exception, that is, of the tiny Philippa: she is not only too young but is still recovering from an attack of polio the previous year.

Len, by this time, is finishing her second year as head girl – and a remarkably successful and popular one she is; Margot is games prefect – still a colourful personality but all round a reformed character; Con is not only a prefect but the editor of the school's magazine, the "Chaletian". ("'By the way . . . [the speaker is Miss Annersley] . . . you're following in your mother's footsteps. She was our first editor. I know she'll be thrilled to hear that you are the twenty-fifth.'")

Felicity, as flaxen-haired as ever, is now quite a seasoned member of the Junior School and has ambitions to take up ballet. Cecil, who like Con and Charles is very dark in colouring, has just graduated from the Kindergarten to the Chalet School proper when the triplets begin their final term.

As to the boys, they all – again with one exception in little Geoffrey, Philippa's twin – attend boarding schools in England; presumably following the same path as their father and uncles, for although we are told no details about Jack Maynard's education, nor about that of Jem Russell or Dick Bettany, we can hazard a guess that all three went to English public schools.

With nine of the children away at school, there were plainly gaps at Freudesheim during term-time. Of course the house was separated from the Chalet School by only a garden's length, and the Chalet girls, both relatives and otherwise, are always in and out. The staff, too, quite often run over for a chat and some of Anna's delicious biscuits. Not to mention the streams of visitors who arrive continually.

In any case, even without resorting to quadruplets, warm-hearted Joey has many ways of enlarging the family group. Already, a couple of years before that conversation with Grizel Cochrane, recorded above, she and Jack had become guardians to, and indeed adopted, the three Richardsons – Ruey (full name

Ruhanna), Roger and Roddy. And during the year of the school's twenty-fifth birthday celebrations, two more children were to be adopted: little Claire Mabillon – a baby abandoned when her mother was killed in a train crash; and Erica Standish, a twelve-year-old orphan from Coorg in India. The latter provides some interesting links with Jo's early life and with the missing book, *Two Chalet Girls in India* (see Questions). For it turns out that Jo had known Erica's mother, then Dacia Parsons; and, as she explains at her dramatic first meeting with Erica, "'[Dacia and I] were great pals in Coorg . . . [That was when] I was packed off [to India] together with young Robin . . . Oh, won't *she* be thrilled to hear about all this! Rob was awfully fond of your mother.'"

For that matter, Robin Humphries is yet another who must be included within the Maynards' extended family: from soon after the time she arrived at the Chalet School as a motherless six-year-old, Robin had been Joey's adopted sister and the two had always been especially close.

Nor should others be forgotten, who at various times had found a home with Jo and her family. Among them – in the earlier days, Daisy and Primula Venables, orphan daughters of Jem Russell's sister Margot Venables; the Macdonald twins, Flora and Fiona (nicknamed naughtily by Jo "Flora and Fauna"); Frieda von Ahlen, formerly Mensch, and her children; and of course Elisaveta, who was once "The Princess of the Chalet School". In later years, Mary-Lou Trelawney (an important honorary member of the household) . . . Adrienne Desmoines and Melanie Lucas . . . the list could go on . . .

No doubt about it – Freudesheim, like Joey's previous houses with their wonderfully elastic capacity, must have been not only a happy home but a hummingly busy one.

SHORT STORY

The Triumvirate Went Ski-ing

"I wish we could go ski-ing as you used to in Tirol,
Daisy!" Beth Chester cast a wistful glance out of the
window of the Third Form room, where she and her
two chums, known in the Chalet School as the
triumvirate, were sitting. They were alone, for once,
as the rest were in the gym, drearily undergoing
extra drill for sins committed. For a wonder none of
the three had been involved, though that, as Daisy
Venables had sagely remarked five minutes before,
was more by good luck than good management.
Daisy herself had been at a music lesson, and Beth
and Gwensi Howell, the third member of the party,
had been upstairs, ordered there by Matron, to
remake their beds *properly*! They had growled at the
time; but just now they had been pluming themselves
on having escaped the twenty minutes of "arms-
bend-and-stretch" and all the other boring exercises.
This extra drill was the lot of the rest daily for the
next week as a punishment for putting a live mouse
into the form mistress's desk.

Now Daisy followed Beth's glance, and shivered. "What awful weather! I don't call this winter at all. There'll be snow in Tirol by this time. Just look at that rain!"

They looked. The pitless December rain was coming down as if it never meant to stop; the garden with its empty border, bare shrubs and trees, and great expanse of sodden lawn, looked mournful in the extreme.

"It's ghastly!" said Beth, brought up in Guernsey, and unaccustomed to this icy rain which made everything look so miserable. Daisy, born in Australia, and then brought to the Tirol four years ago, was also unused to the deluge that pours down in the west Midlands, and her rosy face lengthened perceptibly.

Gwensi chuckled. "Don't you worry, you two. We'll have all the snow you want before winter is over! Megan was telling me that last month. She said the squirrels had been storing nuts at a great rate, and she hadn't seen so many berries on the bushes, either, since she was a girl, so it was a sure sign of a hard winter."

They cheered up at this. Megan, Gwensi's old nurse, now housekeeper since the removal of the Chalet School from Guernsey to the Golden Valley in Armishire, was a mine of country lore. As her prophecies came true about four times out of ten, the triumvirate devoutly believed in all she said. It followed that if Megan had said there would be snow, snow there would be!

However, they had no time for more talk, for

there came the clatter of feet, and the rest of the form arrived, very cross, and rather out of breath, since Miss Nalder had kept them hard at it. The three separated, to go to their own desks and sympathise with the others.

"But it was a mad thing to do," said Daisy severely. "You might have known Ma'mselle would make a fuss. And what did you get out of it anyhow? She didn't yell or jump on a chair – only got furious!"

"Whose idiot idea was it?" asked Beth curiously.

"Margaret Anstey's," said Doris Hamblin, a pretty, fair child, who was generally law-abiding enough, but who had been drawn into this last escapade with the rest.

Margaret chuckled. "We did it at our last school, Mary and I. Ma'mselle there simply yelled. I thought it would be fun."

"Well, now you know it isn't!" retorted Doris sharply. "You'd better have another think the next time you want to play tricks on anyone *here*!"

A bell ringing at that moment brought these recriminations to an abrupt end. It was the first tea-bell, and they all had to hurry to the Splasheries to wash their hands and tidy their hair, for the second bell was due to ring ten minutes later.

The rain continued all that night and next day; but the day after, it ceased, the wind veered to the north, bringing with it a nip that made the less hardy members of the school shiver. The next morning saw a heavy frost, and towards afternoon flakes of snow began to drift down. No one paid much heed to them, for the school at large was busy preparing for its Christmas concert. A big rehearsal had been called for two o'clock in Hall.

But the snow, having begun, seemed determined to keep on, and fell heavily for two days, at which time it ended, though the lowering skies, heavy with clouds that seemed to rest along the summits of the Welsh hills not so far away, gave promise of more to come.

It was Saturday. When letter-writing and mending were ended, one or two of the Thirds found themselves with time on their hands until the bell should ring for "Elevenses", which preceded the Guide meeting. Among these were Daisy and Beth – Gwensi was still struggling with an enormous hole in the heel of a stocking – and they strolled over to one of the windows, while the others clustered round the big log fire burning on the hearth.

"There's *snow*, anyhow," said Beth, harking back to the talk of a few days before. "Could we ski on this, Daisy?"

Daisy shook her head. "No; it's soft, and you want frost before it's fit for ski-ing. If it would freeze it might be all right. I like this," she added cheerfully. "It reminds me of Tirol."

"P'raps it'll freeze tonight," said Beth hopefully.

"We could ski tomorrow if it froze like glass. It's Sunday."

"What's that about Sunday?" asked Doris, who had come to join them.

"Bethy wants to ski, but I told her we couldn't on *that* snow," said Daisy, waving a hand toward the window. "It'll have to freeze first. And even if it

79

froze tonight, we couldn't exactly ski tomorrow."

Doris looked wistful. "I heard lots about ski-ing when we were in Switzerland for our holidays two years ago. But that was the summer. It sounded awful fun, though. D'you think they'd let us try if the snow held out till Monday? We couldn't play netball, anyhow."

"Where are you going to get the skis?" asked Daisy sensibly.

"Couldn't we make them? They're only long bits of wood coming to a point at one end, aren't they?" said Beth.

"Not real skis. I think they're made of cane. But I dare say we could manage something. I wonder if we could?" Daisy's fresh face grew thoughtful. "It would be lovely fun. I haven't skied since we left the Tiernsee, and not much there. But sometimes we used to spend part of the Christmas holidays with Frieda Mensch – Mrs von Ahlen, you know – in Innsbruck, and they have it there. I'd love to try again!"

"Let's go and ask the Head," suggested Beth.

"No go! She'd be sure to think we'd kill ourselves or break something," said Doris. "I remember some-one told Daddy of a bad accident on the – the Cresta Run, I think it was."

Daisy nodded. "Yes, that's true. We'd better say nothing – not yet, anyhow. Look here!" she added. "I'm going home this afternoon till Monday. I'll look in the attic and see if our skis came with us. I don't know; I've never seen them. But they *may* be there. If they are, I'll ask Jo if I can bring them. If not,

we'll get hold of some wood and see if we can't make
something that'll do instead. I don't think it'd be
dangerous just messing about on the hills here. The
big runs in Switzerland are purposely made difficult
for the racing. We didn't hurt ourselves at Innsbruck
– or not much, anyhow, just bruises."

"Shall you tell the others?" asked Beth.

"I think not. We couldn't manage skis for everyone. Just us three – and Doris, as she's heard of it,"
she added. "D'you want to try, Dorry? Right, then;
just us four. Don't let the others hear a word."

They promised fervently, and Daisy was able to
get hold of Gwensi alone later on, and tell her what
was in the wind. Gwensi agreed enthusiastically. She
was fond of games of all kinds, and had been fired
by Daisy's tales of their doings in Tirol.

At half-past two Daisy's "aunt-by-marriage", to
quote herself and Daisy, otherwise Joey Maynard,
came to take Daisy home for the weekend, and the
small girl set off determined to have a good rummage
in the attic at Plas Gwyn for the coveted skis.

Daisy returned to school on Monday empty-
handed. Tactful questions had given her the information that the skis had been left behind, with a
good many other things not considered necessary,
when the school had left Tirol. But she had also
learned from Jo one or two facts that she had not
known before. Hansi, who had been boy-of-all-work
at the Tiernsee, had manufactured skis from pine-
branches, and had learned to skim in all directions
on them, while Jo had, on one occasion, spliced the
blades of two broken oars to pieces of board, and

contrived to move about on those!

"I wouldn't call it ski-ing exactly, though," she added with one of her infectious grins.

"We can do as well as that!" thought Daisy, strictly to herself.

Fresh snow had fallen on the Sunday, but the night had been cloudless, with hard frost, and the roads were like glass. All cars had chains, and Daisy herself was late for Prayers, as Jo dared not drive with any sort of speed.

As a result of this, it was not till Break that Daisy was able to get her friends by themselves in a quiet corner, and tell them her news.

"It's a nuisance the skis were left behind," she finished up, "but if Hansi could make some, I'm jolly sure we could. He was awfully nice, but he wasn't – well – *bright*!"

"Of course we can!" Beth, sister of brothers and child of a large family where they often had to "make do", was not in the least dismayed at the prospect, and Gwensi and Doris accepted her word for it.

"We'll have to scout round for wood," said Doris. "Luckily, as all games are off, we shall have time. The Head said at Prayers this morning that we could all go out and play in the garden this afteroon so long as we wrapped up and kept moving about."

"Then we four can have a shot at the woodshed and see if we can find anything suitable," decided Daisy. "Bother! There goes the bell! I say, Doris, have you got cold?" she added, as that young lady suddenly began to sneeze.

"Oh no!" said Doris hastily. "Just a sneezelum!"

But by dinner-time it was all too plain that she had indeed caught cold somehow, and she was removed to sick-room by a vigilant Matey, who saw no reason why she should be allowed to spread the infection.

The other three pitied her when they were alone, but agreed that it might be as well if they could experiment by themselves first.

"Poor old Dorry! She's awfully delicate, you know," said Beth. "She might have made her cold heaps worse. But this weather looks as if it would last a bit, so I expect she'll get plenty of chances. Now remember, you two, slip off to the woodshed as soon as it's safe. If we get those things made today, we can try them tomorrow."

"Rather!" said Daisy. "This is going to last for a *few* days, anyway."

It proved a fairly easy matter to "slip off", and the trio made straight for the woodshed, where they were lucky in finding none of the men about. Before long, Daisy had rooted out some long, narrow strips of thin board, sufficiently pliant to make them hopeful of curving one end properly. All three possessed Scout knives of great sharpness, and they soon had the boards sliced down to what Daisy thought was about the right width.

"How do we keep them on?" demanded Beth when they had got thus far.

"We must bore holes and put straps through," said Daisy, ceasing from her labours to push back one yellow plait which had fallen over her shoulder.

"Luckily, that pricker thing in our knives will just do the trick."

"We'll have to go carefully, then, in case we split the wood," said Gwensi. "Look here, what about heating one of them and *burning* the holes through? Evan Evans has left his oil-stove here." And she pointed to the little Beatrice that stood on a near-by bench.

"Good scheme!" agreed Beth heartily. "Come on, Daisy!"

At the expense of some bad scorch-marks on the wood, one of Daisy's mittens, and a horrid smell, they got it done eventually. Some old leather lying in the shed yielded straps, and their skis were beginning to look quite "professional" – only the turned-up points proved beyond their powers.

"We'll just have to do without them!" declared Daisy, after sundry fruitless experiments. "I don't suppose it really matters much anyhow. Probably it's just done for the look of the thing."

"There's the bell ringing! We'll have to go!" added Beth. "Shove them into this corner so that nobody sees them, and come on!"

The "skis" were hastily thrust into a far corner, and then the three, hot, dirty, and rather weary after their work, raced to the great mansion, and were soon mingling with their companions.

"I say, where did you three get to this afternoon?" asked Mary Anstey inquisitively as they all streamed in to tea.

"Nowhere! We were about all the time," said Gwensi sharply.

This was true, for she herself had insisted that only two of them at a time must be in the woodshed. The third must be about the shrubbery or lawn in case any prefects took it into their heads to miss them. The other two would not have bothered themselves about such a matter, but Gwensi was a far-sighted young person.

"Well, I scarcely saw any of you," declared Mary. Then they had to separate, as they sat at different tables.

Thanks to Gwensi, no one had missed them, and no one said anything more to them. They hugged themselves as they remembered those three pairs of "skis" with their pointed ends and straps ready for the morrow. It is to be feared that not one of them did much during preparation, and sundry mistresses had good reason for their scathing remarks in form next day. Little the triumvirate cared for that! The frost and the snow had both held; games were "off" again; and that afternoon they meant to SKI!

It almost seemed as if Fate were in league with them. After dinner the Head sent for Daisy to ask her to take a basket of things up to the little cottage on the far side of the hill against which Plas Howell was built. The small daughter of one of the Plas Howell men had come home two days before from the hospital in Armiford after an appendix operation, and the kindly Head Mistress knew that the time would pass slowly for little Joy, and a new story-book, a jigsaw puzzle, a game, and some dainties would help her along.

"May Beth and Gwensi come with me, please?" asked Daisy.

"Well, I shouldn't send you alone," smiled Miss Annersley. "Yes, you may all three go. Girls as old as you should be able to do a simple message without getting into mischief," she added. "Straight there and straight back, please, Daisy. I want you in the garden before twilight comes, remember."

Then she dismissed the long-legged schoolgirl with the basket, and Daisy, shaking with excitement, went off to summon Beth and Gwensi, and tell them what had happened.

"How're we to manage about the skis, though?" asked Beth.

"That's easy! We've got to go through the shrubbery, so we pass the shed. Gwen and I shall keep on slowly, and you can slip in and get them. We'll take them to the top of the hill and leave them there. Then we'll deliver the basket for Joy, and try them out as we come home. We'll be doing just what we were told, so *that's* all right, and we'll never get such a good chance again." Thus Daisy!

The other two agreed with her that it was an excellent opportunity, and no one's conscience troubled her in the least as they set off, walking demurely through the shrubbery. Beth cast a hurried glance behind her to be sure that no one was watching. When they reached the shed she dived in while the other two went on, and soon caught up with them, her arms full of the unwieldy things they had made.

"We'd better hurry a bit. I thought I heard someone coming this way!" she panted. "Here, take your own!"

They took them, and went, chattering eagerly of the fun they were going to have, the other two plying Daisy with questions as to her Innsbruck experiences.

They had to spend at least half an hour at the cottage, for Joy, a child of their own age, was lonely, as her mother was busy and her brothers and sisters were out all day. She wanted to talk. But at length they got away, and set off at top speed for the corner where they had concealed the skis. Arrived there, they put them on, and then Daisy, as the only experienced one, tried to glide forward. But she soon found that ski-ing on proper skis, with balancing poles to help, was quite a different thing from trying to ski on their very home-made affairs with no support whatever. She had been proficient when they left Tirol, but she was out of practice, and those queer things felt very different from the light cane skis she had formerly used. She made two steps forward, and then sat down violently. The other two rushed to pick her up, and did the same thing.

"Ow! That hurts!" cried Gwensi, rubbing herself.

"Oh, it always happens just at the beginning," said Daisy with an air. "Anyhow, we're not really on the crest of the hill. Let's take them off and wait till we get there. And when we start again, try to turn your feet out so that the points don't get across each other. I ought to have told you that before."

They slipped the things off, and went on for the hundred yards or so before they reached the crest of the hill. Again they put their "implements" on. Daisy glanced down the steep slope, and a little misgiving crept into her mind. But already Beth, always the most daring of the three, was preparing to get off, so she repressed her doubts, and with a final "Now, be careful about your points!" was away.

They had reached the cottage by a path dug by the men; but at this part no path existed. The snow was like glass with the hard frost. Before she could stop herself, Daisy was flying down the hill at a speed she had not imagined before. She tried to keep her head, and spread out her arms to retain her balance. Gwensi watched her, and did the same thing. Beth, more heedless, set off without any precautions, and paid the price of her carelessness. Her points seemed to rush together, despite all she could do, and she turned a wild somersault, coming down violently on one shoulder, and then sliding in a sitting position down the slippery slope, till she was able to hook her other arm round a young tree standing near and stop herself.

As for Daisy and Gwensi, they retained their upright position, but both were terrified at what was happening. To Daisy it seemed as if she must crash direct into the brick wall that surrounded the Plas Howell garden. Mercifully, this did not happen, or there might have been a tragedy. She caught one point on a boulder which rose well above the surface of the hill, and went head over heels into a ditch. She was bruised and scratched, but no serious damage had been done.

Gwensi, on the other hand, with natural balance,

and a sudden sheer delight in the movement through the air, kept her head, contrived to describe an arc as she neared the garden wall, and saved herself from any harm at all. Then she took off her "skis," and tried to climb back to Daisy's help.

All in all, it was an exciting time, and it took them a good while to collect Beth, whose shoulder was hurting her badly, and get her down to Plas Howell. By that time the world was shadowed by grey twilight, and Miss Wilson had come to the gate to look for them, as they had not come in with the others.

Her face when she saw them and their "skis" was a study. None of the three ever knew how much she longed to laugh. Evan Evans, who was also there, uttered many exclamations in Welsh as he picked up the half-fainting Beth – she had bruised her collarbone badly – and carried her to sick-room, where Matey took her in hand. The other two were ushered by a grim-looking Miss Wilson into the Head's presence and left to their fate. And Fate was not kind now.

Miss Annersley reproached them with being underhand, for, as she said, they knew very well that she would never have allowed such wild doings, nor even permitted them to go alone if she had not trusted them; and they had betrayed her trust.

At this point Daisy, whose bruises and scratches were stinging and aching, began to cry, and Gwensi was not long in following her example. Miss Annersley was not severe. She was reproachful, and that was ten times worse. Finally she handed them over to Matron with the knowledge that they would not soon be trusted again, and the further punishment of missing the usual Saturday night dancing and fun. Instead, they would go to bed after supper.

For the rest of the term the three were completely subdued, and very meek. No one but Doris was ever told what had really happened, and she held her tongue loyally, even though she would now not have any chance of trying her hand at ski-ing. Not that Nature would have permitted it then. Two days after the escapade the thaw came, and it remained till the end of term. As for Beth, the pain of her collar-bone stayed in her memory for a long time, and acted as a brake on any more mad tricks.

"But," said Miss Wilson to a select audience of the Head and Joey Bettany, "I would have given a good deal to have seen the beginning of that affair!"

"I'm thankful I *didn't*!" said Miss Annersley.

"It's a glad new episode for my latest book," quoth Jo the Writer.

THE FIRST MEMBERS OF THE CHALET SCHOOL

STAFF and *PUPILS*

MISS MADGE BETTANY	Headmistress and founder of the school
MADEMOISELLE LEPATTRE	Madge's partner and assistant

JO BETTANY	
GRIZEL COCHRANE	have all arrived before the school opens
SIMONE LECOUTIER	

GISELA MARANI	
BERNHILDA MENSCH	
FRIEDA MENSCH	all arrive on the first day
BETTE RINCINI	
GERTRUD STEINBRUCKE	
MARIA MARANI	

MARGARET DAPHNE BETTANY (always called *Madge*) – later *Mrs James RUSSELL*; (and, some years afterwards, *Lady Russell*).

Madge Bettany is not quite twenty-five when she takes the momentous decision to run a school. She and Dick, her twin brother, and their twelve-year-old sister Joey have been orphans for many years, and their elderly guardian has died just before the opening of the first story. Dick is working in the Indian Forestry Department, and Madge has to find some way of supplementing the family's small private income that will enable her and Joey to remain together. The school is Madge's solution to this problem. And she chooses to begin her venture in the Tirol because, in those days, it was possible to live in Austria "for next to nothing". (Incredible as this may appear today, at the time when *The School at the Chalet* was written it would have been perfectly true.)

Madge has no experience of teaching, and only a tiny amount of capital. But she does not lack courage, and plainly was born under a lucky star. Not that her success is due to good fortune alone, for Madge has considerable gifts of personality. Despite being on the young side for a headmistress, she is able to command not only the respect but the loyalty and affection of staff, pupils and parents alike. And it is largely due to her vitality and enthusiasm that the Chalet School flourishes from the beginning.

"Madame" – as Madge is always called in the school, this being a title familiar to most of the nations represented – is greatly missed when she marries Doctor James Russell and goes to live on the Sonnalpe. After this, in accordance with the ideas of the time, she has to give up her teaching, apart from the occasional visit. But she continues through the years to own the school and to keep a close connection with it, being always consulted on any matters of importance.

Her own children are not slow to begin arriving: David, the eldest son, is born less than a year after the wedding, and is followed twenty-one months later by a daughter who is given the names Sybil Margaret. Two more daughters, Josette and Ailie, appear at somewhat wider intervals; and finally, after several years' gap, twins – Kevin and Kester – arrive to complete the Russell family.

Many Chalet fans have regretted that Madge leaves the centre of the stage after only two years and a term. True, she does continue to play a significant role during the years before Joey grows up, and she always remains in sight; but once immersed in domesticity Madge does not impinge to the same extent. In the early books, she comes over as quite a convincing adult, one of the few to be found in school stories of the period.

MADEMOISELLE LEPÂTTRE – *Thérèse Elise*
(But see Questions section)

Before the series begins, Mademoiselle has been working as a governess in Taverton, the town where the Bettanys have their home in the early chapters of *The School at the Chalet*. She is not happy in her post and hence is delighted to become Madge's partner in her plan to establish the Chalet School. We are not told Mademoiselle's age but it is plain she is very much older than the twenty-four-year-old Madge – Dick Bettany takes some comfort from knowing there will be someone around of more mature years to keep an eye on his sisters.

For Mademoiselle, one attraction of the scheme lies in the opportunity it affords for her little cousin Simone Lecoutier (q.v.) whose family are not well off, to receive a free education. And Mademoiselle proves to be an ideal partner in Madge's enterprise. Not only does she undertake the teaching of French, German, and Needlework, she provides a steady supply of practical commonsense advice, and is consistently supportive to her young headmistress.

Not surprisingly, when Madge marries and has to relinquish her role as acting head of the Chalet School, Mademoiselle Lepâttre is considered her natural successor. She carries out the duties of headmistress most effectively, and although she does not have a highly colourful personality, her genuine kindness and sound no-nonsense approach earn her the school's respect and growing affection. Girls and fellow members of staff are devastated when, about three and a half years after being appointed head-mistress, Mademoiselle is taken seriously ill. At first everyone hopes she will soon be restored to health. But when, a couple of terms later, it becomes clear that she is if anything going downhill, her position as headmistress has to be taken by Miss Annersley.

A while later it transpires that Mademoiselle has now become a complete invalid. Hence, when the news of her death is announced – during the school's first term in Guernsey – the sorrow this brings is mingled with relief that her long illness is over.

JOSEPHINE MARY BETTANY (known as *Jo*, or *Joey*) – later *Mrs Jack MAYNARD*

Jo becomes the Chalet School's first pupil, and she is unquestionably the most important character in the series. In the opening story she is a lively twelve-year-old with "at least five times as much spirit as strength" whose health at this point often gives cause for anxiety; and it is partly in order that her younger sister may benefit from mountain air, that Madge chooses for her school a location three thousand feet above sea level.

In the "dry life-giving air of the Tirolean alps" Joey's health improves rapidly. And although her propensity for launching into hazardous escapades lands her in a couple of dramatic illnesses, plus a handful of lesser ones, she eventually grows up to become, if not exactly robust, most certainly resilient.

As a schoolgirl, Jo is portrayed with quite a realistic mixture of good qualities and faults. Maybe she does have an extra lavish helping of gifts – among them, a sensitive imagination, great promise as a writer, a beautiful singing voice, and of course a warm heart and a charismatic personality. On the other hand, she is capable of being moody, is often impatient and at times sarcastic, even snappy when provoked. Into the bargain she is extremely untidy, and impulsive to the point of rashness. It all adds up to a convincing and attractive presentation which, in the early books, is always seasoned with a touch of humour.

Through most of her schooldays, Joey shows a marked resistance to the idea of growing up, and even stages an outright protest when told she has been appointed as the Chalet School's head girl. But during her final year her attitude begins to change a little. Then, later on, the harrowing experiences she endures during – and before – the escape from Austria, help to speed the maturing process. And despite the protests she has always made about remaining the family's permanent maiden aunt, Joey, by the time she is twenty, has married Jack Maynard, one of the doctors at the Sanatorium on the Sonnalpe (see article on the Maynard family, page 61).

A year or so later her family is inaugurated in characteristically startling fashion, by the arrival of triplet daughters. The Maynards are to be a long family: the total by the forty-eighth book of the series has reached eleven – six girls and five boys – and Joey is even threatening, perhaps not altogether seriously, to top up with quadruplets! Nevertheless, the demands of family life are not allowed to engulf Jo's irrepressibly youthful spirits. She insists that she will always remain a Chalet girl at heart, even when she's "a great grandmother in a bath chair". And in addition to her duties as mother of eleven, and joint guardian with her husband to several wards, she finds time to be a highly successful writer. Not to mention that she continues to play the roles of counsellor, comforter, champion "butter-in" and straightener-out of problems – both within and outside the Chalet School – to the very end of the series.

Jo Bettany/Maynard is unmistakably Elinor Brent-Dyer's own favourite among her enormous roll-call of Chalet School characters. Yet, interestingly, in a school where the majority of girls are pretty, and some outstandingly lovely, Jo is among the few with no claims to beauty. This Elinor makes clear from the first moment Jo appears on the scene. At this point, Jo's short black hair, cut with an uncompromisingly square fringe, was "so straight as almost to be described as lank; her big black eyes made the intense whiteness of her face even more startling than it need have been, and her cheeks and temples were hollow with continual ill-health". And although before too long the "warm sun and clean mountain air" in the Tirol have "wiped out the unnatural pallor", with the result that Joey has "begun to lose her goblin-like appearance", we are still being told that "Pretty, she would never be". This, however, serves only to emphasise the close link between Jo and her creator; for Elinor herself was considered plain as a child, and it seems she was not altogether indifferent to her lack of beauty. And, in portraying Jo's appearance (so well captured in Nina Brisley's illustrations for the early hardback editions) as "distinctive", or "full of character", but never in the least pretty, Elinor was almost certainly identifying with her best-loved heroine.

GRIZEL COCHRANE – Later (much later) *Mrs Neil SHEPPARD*

Grizel is accounted the second of the Chalet School's pupils, but in fact she is the first from outside the family. She is an only child, and her life at home with an unsympathetic stepmother and a father who shows little interest in her, has not been a happy one. Hence fourteen-year-old Grizel is only too delighted at the prospect of leaving home and going to school abroad. She is nice-looking and intelligent, excels in most athletic pursuits, and is full of energy and enthusiasm. In many ways it appears she will prove an ideal schoolgirl; but there is "a certain hardness in her character" (frequently mentioned), which is partly the result of her home background. The latter has also produced in Grizel a rather narrow outlook; and since she is extremely head-strong, has little sense of humour and not much imagination, Grizel at first encounters many problems in school life. Gradually she settles down and learns to fit in with the others; and eventually, during her last two terms at the Chalet School, she is promoted to be head girl. This brings out the best in her, and for a while she blossoms. But her cherished ambition to become a teacher of gym and PE is thwarted by her father's insistence – and he holds the purse-strings – that Grizel study music in Italy. Later, after a period of enforced study in Florence, she returns to the Chalet School to teach the piano. Later still she goes to spend some years in New Zealand. But things never seem to work out right for poor old Grizel. Until, anyway, the forty-fourth book of the series, when she is finally allowed to find happiness in marriage to a doctor – Elinor's ultimate reward for any good Chalet School girl.

Grizel is always most insistent that her name should be pronounced with the stress on the second syllable – and not as in the word "grizzle".

SIMONE LECOUTIER –
Later *Mrs André de BERSAC*

Simone, cousin of Mademoiselle Lepattre (q.v.) is the third member of the Chalet School's original trio. She is twelve years old in the opening story, has never before been away from her family in France, and at first she is dreadfully homesick. This, combined with the strong vein of jealousy in her nature, causes her to be extremely unhappy during her early days at the Chalet School. In addition, Simone is desperately anxious to be "best friends" on an exclusive basis with Joey; and the latter finds the French girl's sentimental attitude altogether too sloppy. Matters are not helped, either, by Simone's tendency to burst into tears without very much provocation. However, as the years go by, things change. Simone gradually adjusts to the Chalet School way of life;

she learns to "brace up" and to avoid being over-demonstrative. And in the course of time she is indeed to become one of Joey's closest friends; not only throughout their schooldays but to the end of the series.

Simone is another old girl of the school who returns to teach there. But, unlike Grizel Cochrane, she marries at the not too advanced age of about twenty-three, and eventually produces a number of children, the eldest being named Thérèse Elise after Mademoiselle Lepâttre.

GISELA MARANI –
Later Mrs Gottfried MENSCH

Gisela, at sixteen, is the oldest of the six Tirolean girls who arrive to join the Chalet School on its first morning. In appearance, she is very dark, slightly built and graceful. In personality she quickly proves herself to be reliable, kind, and mature for her years; so not surprisingly she is chosen to be the Chalet School's first head girl – an office which she fills with quiet efficiency.

Gisela spends only four terms at the Chalet School but she always remains in close touch. Her unobtrusive influence continues to be felt even after her marriage to Doctor Gottfried Mensch – brother of Bernhilda and Frieda – who is another member of the medical team at the Sanatorium on the Sonnalpe.

Gisela and Gottfried's eldest daughter, Natalie, is described by Joey as "the Chalet School's first grandchild". In due course she and all Gisela's other daughters become pupils at the Chalet School.

BERNHILDA MENSCH –
Later *Mrs Kurt von ESCHENAU*

Bernhilda is the second oldest in the little group of Austrians who join the Chalet School on the first day, and when Gisela is made head girl Miss Bettany appoints Bernhilda as Second Prefect. She and her younger sister, Frieda, are very alike in appearance, both having very long flaxen hair, blue eyes and apple-blossom complexions. At first Bernhilda gives the impression of being only a "well mannered, rather sedate girl", but as her personality develops she often shows great poise; and in a quiet way she exerts a strong influence in the Chalet School during her four terms there.

Bernhilda is another who marries early; and her husband, like Gisela's, is the brother of fellow pupils at the Chalet School – in this case, of Wanda and Marie von Eschenau. (The two von Eschenau girls make the acquaintance of the Chalet School during the first term, but do not enter it officially until the second.) Bernhilda's wedding is described in detail near the beginning of *Eustacia Goes to the Chalet School*. And she too, like so many of the Chalet old girls, settles down to produce a long family.

FRIEDA MENSCH –
Later *Mrs Bruno von AHLEN*

Twelve-year-old Frieda is at first so timid and so completely unobtrusive that for some time she is thought rather colourless by both girls and staff – just "a pale shadow" of her elder sister. But beneath this quiet exterior lies a personality of considerable strength and charm; and in time Frieda develops a character that is anything but negative. Her name, which derives from the German word for Peace, is thought by her schoolfellows to be particularly appropriate, since Frieda is by nature a peace-maker and can always be relied upon to try and smooth over disagreements. Frieda becomes a prefect during Joey's time as head girl and proves herself an invaluable member of the team. Between her and Joey, a specially warm friendship grows. The two are to remain close until the end of the series; and for a time, following her wartime marriage to Doctor Bruno von Ahlen, Frieda makes her home with the Maynards.

At the time the Chalet School opens, Bernhilda and Frieda's parents are living at Seespitz which is not far from the school; and during the summer they come to know the Bettanys on quite an informal basis. Herr Mensch is also able to give Madge advice on several occasions, and a firm friendship is established which leads to an invitation for Madge, Joey and little Robin Humphries to spend Christmas with the Mensch family in Innsbruck. (The second story,

Jo of the Chalet School, gives a delightful account of this Christmas visit.)

BETTE RINCINI –
Later *Mrs di BERSETTI*

Bette is around fifteen at the opening of the series but she has never been to school before, having previously shared a governess at home with Gisela and Maria Marani. However, she soon settles down happily at the Chalet School, and is appointed right away as a sub-prefect. Bette has quite a fiery temperament – attributed to her being half Italian – and exercises a strong influence in the school, where her lively personality and attractive appearance ensure her popularity. Of all the continental girls she is the quickest to perfect her spoken English, which she soon learns to speak idiomatically and with hardly a trace of accent. She also becomes the most expert in written English and is able to contribute a very readable story to the first "Chaletian" magazine.

Bette remains at the school for two and a half years, and in her last term becomes the Chalet School's third head girl. She marries Doctor di Bersetti not long after leaving school, but a few years later is left a widow with two small children when her husband is killed in a mountaineering accident.

GERTRUD STEINBRÜCKE

Gertrud, like Maria Marani, turns up, unofficially, so
to speak, on the opening day at the Chalet School
(of the six Tiroleans who arrive that morning Miss
Bettany had in fact expected only four!). But Gertrud's mother soon appears to formalise the necessary arrangements; and the school gains a pupil who
is thoroughly likeable as well as being sensible and
dependable. Gertrud is soon appointed a sub-
prefect, making the fourth member of the Chalet
School's first team of prefects. She takes part to the
full in all the school's activities and gets on well with
both staff and pupils. In due course she becomes a
full prefect, and during her final two terms takes
over from Grizel Cochrane as Games Captain –
Grizel having just been made head girl.

Not much is heard of Gertrud during the years
following the escape from Austria – she is not among
those who manage to get away from the Tirol. But
around the time of the Chalet School's twenty-first
birthday, Gertrud and another former pupil of the
school have a chance meeting in Salzburg; and as a
result Gertrud is invited to attend one of the school's
celebrations in Switzerland.

MARIA MARANI –
Later *Mrs Walter MACLAREN*

Gisela's little sister Maria is only nine when she first
appears – rather unexpectedly! – at the Chalet

School. Initially she is so quiet and shy that she is hardly noticed; but once she has been joined by other pupils of her own age and even younger, she settles down happily. As the years go by, she becomes in due course a lively and mischievous Middle, then a respected Senior; and finally, during the school's Guernsey days, she is made head girl, following in her elder sister's footsteps.

The last part of Maria's time at school is saddened by the news of her father's death in a Nazi concentration camp. But she has plenty of character, and eventually comes to terms with the tragedy, although she ceases to be a carefree schoolgirl. Her morale improves after she joins the Maynard household to help with Joey's large – and growing – family. But Maria does not become completely her old self until after her engagement and marriage to Walter Maclaren.

A HISTORY OF THE
CHALET SCHOOL

Part One – *The Tirolean Years*

All book numbers referred to are Armada numbers

"Ringed round by mountains, with a long narrow valley stretching away to the west, and water meadows at its southern extremity, the Tiern See in the North Tyrol is surely one of the loveliest places in the world, and an ideal spot for such a school as the Chalet School." Here, Miss Madge Bettany had established her school, "beginning with nine pupils . . ."

In fact there had originally been only three: Joey Bettany, Madge's much younger sister; 14-year-old Grizel Cochrane, who was two years older than Jo but had previously been attending the same school in England; and Simone Lecoutier, cousin of Mademoiselle Lepâttre, the French lady who was Madge Bettany's partner in her brave enterprise. But the Chalet School was destined to be lucky and, by the time the first day arrived, these three had been joined by six Tyrolean girls: Gisela Marani and her little sister Maria; Bernhilda and Frieda Mensch; Bette Rincini and Gertrud Steinbrücke. Gisela, at sixteen the oldest and most responsible of the group, was soon to be chosen by Miss Bettany as the Chalet School's first head girl; and all nine girls, Joey Bettany in particular, were in due course to become pillars of the school and to play roles of some importance throughout the series.

This pattern of steadily growing numbers was always to be a feature of the school's history (with the exception of one short period during the war years). At the end of the first term there were eighteen girls, and the staff had been increased by the arrival of Miss Maynard to teach mathematics; while Herr Anserl, the gruff but golden-hearted Austrian piano professor, had become a regular weekly visitor – two more names that would recur until the end of the series.

By the second term, the total had risen to more than thirty pupils, representing many different nationalities; and new staff included Miss Durrant, who introduces the school to folk dancing, and the eccentric Mr Tristan Denny; the latter would still be taking his inspirational if sometimes hair-raising singing classes more than fifty books later, for he was to follow the school through all its travels.

And so it continued. Despite alarms and excursions – for adventures of many kinds were never lacking at the Chalet School – the numbers went on and on growing. During Joey Bettany's last school year there were upwards of a hundred girls. And the year after that a spectacular increase took place, when the Chalet School joined forces with St Scholastika's – a school situated then on the other side of the Tiernsee, which at one time had been a deadly rival.

After this amalgamation, the "New" Chalet School found itself with nearly 250 pupils and a combined teaching staff so large that another chalet had to be found to house them.

By this time the number of buildings occupied by the school had also increased considerably. The original chalet – "a very large wooden building which had been designed for a hotel" – with its wonderful views of the lake and mountains, was always to be the school's main premises; but, before the second term began, a smaller house was purchased for use by the Juniors. This lay at a short distance from the main school and was known for some years as Le Petit Chalet. A school hall was built during the summer holidays in the third year; laboratories and a domestic economy room were added at various times. Then, just before Joey's last term at school, a new chalet was custom-built in the school grounds: this was designed for the Middle School (those notorious Middles!) and was dedicated to St Clare, the Petit Chalet being now renamed St Agnes's and the original house Ste Thérèse's.

Yet another house was required when the Chalet School absorbed its former rival, and for this new building the name St Scholastika's was retained. The recently acquired staff house, mentioned above, was given the name St Hild's – Madge Russell (the former Miss Bettany) having decreed that an English saint should be honoured this time. Presumably she had in mind St Hilda of Whitby, whose shrine is situated not far from Elinor Brent-Dyer's own child-hood home in the north-east of England.

In addition to all these houses on the original site, there was also the Chalet School Annexe. This – a special unit that had been established on the Son-nalpe (see Locations) during the school's fifth year – catered for particularly delicate children as well as for some whose parents were patients at the nearby Sanatorium. Here the headmistress was Juliet Car-rick, who had been a pupil at the Chalet School during its first two years and was the first old girl to join the staff.

Naturally the school's complement of teachers had also grown steadily as the terms went by. Among important figures who appear early and remain to the end are Miss Wilson, Miss Annersley – she of the beautiful speaking voice and renowned eye-sight – and Matron Lloyd who becomes the school's favourite domestic tyrant; also Miss Stewart, although she disappears after a few years to be married.

Inevitably there were changes. In the school's third year Mademoiselle Lepâttre takes over as headmistress, following Madge Bettany's marriage to Doctor James Russell. (It was Doctor Russell who established the Sanatorium on the Sonnalpe.) But Mademoiselle's reign, successful though it is, does not last long: three years later she is stricken with a serious illness (which eventually proves fatal); and at the beginning of *The New Chalet School* the school learns that Miss Annersley has now been appointed headmistress in her place.

The Chalet School, then, by its final year in the Tirol, had grown in size from just three to about 250 pupils, had a large teaching staff, and was currently occupying six different houses. It had also become a truly international school, at least ten European nations being represented, in addition to the British and several pupils from the United States. As well as being international the school was notably ecumenical in character. There was a strong religious bias but this was deliberately kept non-denominational, with Protestants and Roman Catholics mixing freely on equal terms. In this context, a word is perhaps needed regarding the Chalet School practice of having Catholics and Protestants separated for "Prayers". This may seem odd today, in the 1990s, when the whole school would doubtless have held a joint assembly, whatever their individual religious persuasions. But things were very different at the time the Chalet School began, and Elinor's portrayal of the girls dispersing to separate rooms is entirely authentic.

Traditions were always to be considered important. They, too, were of rapid growth; and by the end of the years in the Tirol the Chalet School way of life was firmly on the lines that have become so familiar to readers. The prefect system, to which Miss Bettany (and plainly Elinor, too) attached great importance, was inaugurated within a few weeks of the school's opening. And from the very beginning, cold baths – from which the girls somehow contrive to emerge "glowing from the icy sting of the mountain water" – were the order of the day; beds had to be meticulously stripped, plumeaus to be aired; and woe betide any girl who had so much as a button missing if Matron's eye should fall on her – as it always did! On the other hand, the school meals were invariably delicious.

No girl should ever have complained of boredom. Before the end of the first year, folk dancing, the Hobbies Club, the school magazine (the "Chaletian"), and much musical activity in addition to choral singing – these were all in full swing. *The Youngest Shepherd*, the first of the annual Christmas plays, had marked thirteen-year-old Joey Bettany's singing debut. Guides and Brownies were started early in the second year. This also saw the founding of the Sanatorium on the Sonnalpe, and the beginning of the hospital's long association with the school. Very soon a Sale of Work in aid of the San becomes an annual event.

Another custom that gets off to an early start is the tireless crusade against the use of slang expressions, a war that is carried on throughout Chalet School history. And during the Christmas term following *The Princess of the Chalet School* (or so it can be deduced – see note on the missing Chalet School books, page 126), those dreaded days are introduced when speaking in French or German is compulsory for all, staff and pupils, lessons and playtimes alike. Presumably the days in between, when only English was allowed, were pretty tough for the other nationalities, although they always seemed to cope rather better.

All these traditions and customs, plus others too numerous to mention, were to endure not only through this early part of Chalet School history but right to the end of the series. They were moreover to survive the many upheavals and migrations that characterise the next phase of the story which begins with *The Chalet School in Exile*.

Part Two – *The Chalet School on the Move*

The opening of *The Chalet School in Exile* sees the first of many changes when the school, after being happily settled at the Tiernsee for between seven and eight years, has to move hurriedly up to the Sonnalpe, following the Nazi annexation of Austria. But this temporary home, in the former hotel Der Edel Ritter, lasts only a few months as the political situation soon makes things impossible. And now for a time the Chalet School ceases to exist. Joey and a handful of the others, who have fallen foul of the Gestapo, make a perilous escape through the mountains to Switzerland, and later to the island of Guernsey.

Here, against all odds, a house is eventually found near Jerbourg. And although numbers at first are reduced to fifty-two, the school gradually struggles back to life. Many old friends from the Tirolean days, both girls and staff, are reunited, including Miss Wilson, Miss Annersley and "Matey"; and Simone Lecoutier and Grizel Cochrane are among old girls who join the teaching staff.

Joey, in the intervening year, has married Jack Maynard, one of the doctors at the Sanatorium (it, too, has removed to Guernsey). And during the first term in Guernsey a major stir is caused by the arrival of Joey's triplet daughters.

Unfortunately the time in Guernsey is short. Once the war starts the Channel Islands can no longer be considered a safe refuge, especially when the Germans look set to occupy the French coast. So yet again the school must be uprooted. But at least this time the new premises they find at Plas Howell in Armishire are to remain their home through the next seven books, and about eight school years. It is here that the custom of having compulsory French and German days is re-introduced – amid a fair amount of groans and grumbles!

School life continues to be filled with activities old and new. Maybe the local hills can hardly compare with the Alps, but there are still energetic walks to be taken, not to mention hop-picking in the fields round about. And one winter some girls manage to commemorate the old Tirolean days by getting lost in the snow. The new interest in gardening, dating from wartime when the Chalet girls had all been encouraged to "Dig for Victory", is steadily maintained and provides material for various escapades.

All round a happy time; but defective drains are found to be causing illness in the school, and yet another move is required.

As always, the school is lucky, and in the nick of time a suitably large house is offered, situated on the island of St Briavel (see Locations). Here, seven of the eight books from No 26 to No 32 inclusive are to be set. The exception is No 30, *The Chalet School in the Oberland*. This describes the school's first venture into Switzerland, when a small group goes to set up a finishing branch, and the events take place during the same term as those at St Briavels which were recounted in No 29, *Shocks for the Chalet School*.

No 32, *Changes for the Chalet School*, paves the way for a last removal – it really is to prove the final one. This time the school's destination is the Görnetz Platz in the Bernese Oberland (see Locations). A number of the girls, including all the Juniors, are to remain in Britain, where they will be housed at Carnbach on the Welsh coast (see Locations); but the end of this book sees about a hundred of the Seniors and Middles all set for travel to Switzerland, and preparing to don a new school uniform in gentian blue.

Throughout the long period of migration the

114

Chalet School has faithfully maintained the traditions and customs that were established during the early years. One new one had been added, one that came about before the escape from Austria: this, the Chalet School Peace League, with its high ideals of international fellowship and understanding, was, like the ecumenical attitude of the school, something considerably in advance of its time.

Part Three – *The Swiss Years*

The third part of the series, comprising books Nos 33 to 62, contains a larger number of books than either of the other two, but covers only about eight school years, with four titles quite often relating to a single year.

The first of the batch, No 33 *Joey Goes to the Oberland*, is not really a school story but is concerned with the Maynard family's long roundabout journey to Switzerland, where they arrive a short time before the school turns up in force. This book leads straight into No 34, *The Chalet School and Barbara*, which provides the first act proper for the school's Swiss drama. But then, somewhat misleadingly, the next book, *Tom Tackles the Chalet School*, is what Elinor would have called a "hop-out-of-kin", since it was published out of chronological order and, despite being originally numbered 31 (in Armada numbering it is 22), belongs in fact to the Armishire part of the series. (See note on *Tom Tackles the Chalet School* and *The Chalet School and Rosalie* in the Questions section.)

After this the stories, from No 35 onwards, follow

each other in correct chronological order. But in three other books the action, for the most part, happens outside Switzerland. These are: No 47, *Joey & Co. in Tirol* and No 51, *A Future Chalet School Girl* – both holiday stories, set mainly in the Tiernsee district, the Chalet School's original home; and No 43, *The Coming of Age of the Chalet School* in which the latter part describes a visit to the Tiernsee by members of the school and various old girls.

For the school, the years in Switzerland prove to be as action-packed as any in their history. The Alpine terrain provides the opportunity for the girls once again to enjoy long walks and scrambles in the clear mountain air; and, with the coming of the snow, to take part in winter sports – a new experience for most.

To begin with, they find that the number of girls has dwindled to a mere hundred or so. But in no time the total starts creeping up again. Three years later there are two hundred girls; and, by the final year of the chronicle, the all-time record has been reached of more than three hundred pupils at the Görnetz Platz, while the branch at Carnbach in Wales has over a hundred.

The staff now includes a greater than ever number of old girls, with Biddy O'Ryan, Peggy Burnett, Rosalie Dean, Hilary Burn and Nancy Wilmot among them at various times. The turnover is fairly rapid, for members of the Chalet School teaching staff often leave to get married – usually to doctors.

Old girls are also represented in a different way

among the pupils, of whom a sizable proportion are now the children of former Chaletians. Joey Bettany/ Maynard and her close friends Frieda, Marie, and Simone, are only a few of those whose daughters appear at the school.

Miss Annersley and Miss Wilson – for some time now joint headmistress – remain to the end. And Joey always manges to find time, despite the demands of her enormous family and busy writing career, to take part enthusiastically in most of the school's activities.

These latter include the traditional half-term excursions, which now range throughout Switzerland; the annual Christmas plays; the staff evenings and form entertainments; and of course the Sales of Work – presented ever more elaborately, and raising ever greater sums of money in aid of the San, which had preceded the school to the Görnetz Platz, and with whom close links were always maintained.

Other traditions, major and minor, are also kept going. The dormitories still have their flower-sprinkled curtains, their plumeaus on the beds, and their all-purpose bureaus. And girls caught using unsuitable slang expressions still have to face heavy, and increasingly far-fetched, penalties.

Mention should also be made of three important events in Chalet School history. Two are fictional: the first, the Chalet School's twenty-first birthday, is marked by extensive celebrations (including the series of visits to the Tiernsee mentioned above) which are described in *The Coming of Age of the*

Chalet School; the second is the school's Silver Jubilee which is among the main themes in *Summer Term at the Chalet School* (1965). The other was an occasion in real life, when the appearance in 1963 of the fiftieth Chalet School book, *The Chalet School Reunion* (numbered 54 in Armada), was celebrated with a large gathering of fans in London and a special presentation to Elinor.

The series ends with the summer term described partly in *Althea Joins the Chalet School* (1969), and partly in *Prefects of the Chalet School* (published posthumously in 1970). This, by coincidence, is also the Maynard triplets' last term at school, and the end of the book sees the three girls headed for university, with one of them already engaged (and naturally to a doctor!).

QUESTIONS AND ANSWERS

Book numbers referred to are the original numbers.

(1) *Did the Chalet School ever exist in real life?*

The stories have described the school so convincingly that readers often assumed the author had a real school in mind; a few simply took this for granted and wrote to ask the publishers for a prospectus! But in fact the Chalet School itself is entirely imaginary. However, its original location in the Tirol does exist, and the school's imagined position there can be pinpointed quite closely. (See Locations.)

(2) *Were any of the characters in the stories real people? – or based on real people? – perhaps the author herself, her friends or relatives?*

Most fictional characters do of course grow from a mixture of the author's imagination and experience; but it seems that none of the Chalet School characters is an exact portrait of any one real-life person. And Elinor Brent-Dyer always denied that she had based any of them on herself or on people she knew. Nevertheless, there can be no question that a great deal of Elinor herself went into her portrayal of Joey Bettany/Maynard. The two have so much in common, despite the obvious differences in their life-styles and physical appearance, that it is clear Elinor must have identified strongly, if unconsciously, with Jo. A very old friend was convinced that "Joey was Elinor herself, as she would have liked to be". And there are traces of real people to be found in several characters. The "Robin", for example, appears to owe something to the child Hazel Bainbridge, for whom Elinor wrote her first published book, although Robin is not actually a portrait of Hazel. Elinor also had a misleading habit of giving her fictional characters the names of people she knew in real life. The most confusing example concerns Madge Russell: this, as every reader will know, is the married name of Madge Bettany who, in fiction, founds the Chalet School. But it was also the name of one of Elinor's real-life friends, to whom she dedicated three books – her Guernsey story *The Maids of La Rochelle*, and both the second and third Chalet School books. Seeing this name printed in the dedications has suggested to many readers that the Madge of the stories really existed. However, no one has been able to trace any connection.

(3)   *Are any of the places in the stories real?*

Yes, many of them are real places, and some are a mixture of real and imaginary; but for a detailed answer to this question see the section on Locations.

(4)   *Why does Mademoiselle change her name?*

It has to be confessed right away that there is no absolutely definite answer to this question! In the first three books, Mademoiselle's surname is La Pâttre – two words and spelt with an "A". In the fourth book, the name has become one word, but still spelt with an "A", viz.: Lapâttre. And through these four books her first name is Elise; at any rate this is the name Madge uses, when addressing her in private. Then all of a sudden, in the fifth book, we find Mademoiselle has now become Lepâttre – one word and spelt with an "E". And the next time a Christian name is mentioned she has become Thérèse. Moreover she continues to be Thérèse until the end. Now Elinor was unquestionably a rather forgetful and disorganised person, but it is hard to believe that during a period of only four years, she could possibly have managed to forget the name she had given to one of her principal characters. Yet, if the change was not a mistake, what possible reason can Elinor have had for making it? No likely explanation comes to mind. And the mystery has never been solved. Although it seems the discrepancy must have been pointed out to Elinor, for she stages a kind of salvage operation in *Jo to the Rescue*; here,

Simone introduces her daughter as "Thérèse Elise – after a cousin who died". And full marks to Elinor for ingenuity, even if this still leaves unexplained the matter of La Pâttre/Lapâttre/Lepâttre.

(5)   *Which of the Matrons is the real "Matey"? – sometimes she seems to be Lloyd, sometimes Gould, and at least once Rider . . .*

This, which is similar to the previous question, has also caused endless confusion. But here it is possible to straighten things out by referring to the books – and keeping a cool head. And, weighing one thing with another, it can be established that the real "Matey" who first appears in the missing story that precedes *Head Girl of the Chalet School* (see reply to question (8)), is quite definitely Matron Gwynneth *Lloyd*. For one thing, Matron Gould, who joins the school later and takes charge of the Juniors, "stood five foot eleven in her stockings", whereas "Matey" is small and wiry. Both Matrons, Lloyd and Gould, are mentioned by name in *Jo Returns to the Chalet School*, making clear that they are two different people. Then Matron Rider belongs originally to St Scholastika's School and joins the Chalet School staff only when the two schools merge. As to why the confusion happens, the answer must be the same as to question (4) above. These two queries open up the whole intriguing matter of inconsistencies in the Chalet School series, which will be dealt with later.

(6) *Why did the Chalet School never return to the Tirol?*

This may be answered on two levels. In the stories various reasons are given, including the post-war international situation; (and it is true that the Peace Treaty with Austria was not signed until 1955 and that, with the country still occupied by the Allied forces, this would have made it difficult for an international school to settle in the Tirol). It is also stated in various books that the level of water in the "Tiernsee" had risen, following the construction of a dam at the head of the lake, and that this had flooded some of the land round the original school – not in fact the case in real life. Yet another problem is mentioned: the Water Board is said to have taken over the chalet where the school began – and most likely all the other buildings as well. But the fact of the matter is that Elinor probably wanted the greater freedom she enjoyed when her school was placed in an imaginary situation. She was then able to describe the scenery and topography quite freely; and if she wanted to make adjustments or additions in order to fit the stories, she could do this without fearing that someone who knew the district might point out the discrepancies. This had begun to happen at times in the past, once people discovered the real identity of the "Tiernsee". And by creating the entirely fictional Görnetz Platz for the school, while continuing to use her beloved Tirolean setting from time to time in holiday stories, Elinor contrived to have the best of two worlds.

(7)   *Are any of Elinor Brent-Dyer's other books connected with the Chalet School series?*

There are three points in particular where the Chalet School's path is joined by that of other Brent-Dyer stories. The first – in *The Chalet School in Exile* – occurs when the school starts up in Guernsey, and three families are introduced: the Chesters, the Lucys, and the Ozannes, who all come from the so-called "La Rochelle" series (family stories, set mainly in Guernsey). Other characters from "La Rochelle" who arrive at the Chalet School in due course include members of the Willoughby and Eltringham families. Then in *The Chalet School at War* (originally *The Chalet School Goes To It*) the new girls arriving at the beginning of term include Monica Marillar and some of her friends from Medbury, who first appeared in a school story Elinor wrote in the 1930s called *Monica Turns up Trumps*. And in *Lavender Leigh at the Chalet School* (originally *Lavender Laughs in the Chalet School*) two of the new Seniors are characters from *The Lost Staircase* named Jesanne Gellibrand and Lois Bennett.

(8)   *Are there any books missing from the Chalet School series?*

This question is usually asked in connection either with certain gaps between the stories, or with Joey's visit to India which is mentioned in a number of the later books though not apparently related in any of the early ones. In fact Elinor did write a full-length book about the adventures of Joey and Robin Humphries when they went to India to visit Jo's brother, Dick Bettany, and his family. The manuscript was known still to exist in the late 1950s, but unfortunately the book was never published and the manuscript has now disappeared. This story, *Two Chalet Girls in India*, would have filled a gap that lies between *The New Chalet School* and *The Chalet School in Exile*. The other missing book is one that should have come between *The Princess of the Chalet School* and *The Head Girl of the Chalet School*, where a whole term elapses. Elinor never completed a book about this particular term, but she did leave clear indications of the form the story would have taken, along with some notes about the plot, so it has been possible to reconstruct the story although it too remains unpublished. Of the other gaps that exist in the series, one – that between the second and third books – extends to a whole year. And it can be deduced, using the children's ages as a guide, that at the opening of *Three Go to the Chalet School* about three years have passed since the end of the previous story (*The Chalet School and Rosalie*). But it seems clear that neither of these gaps was ever filled.

(9) *Was the school where Elinor Brent-Dyer herself went as a child at all like the Chalet School?*

Both No and Yes to this. Elinor attended a small private day-school in South Shields, which had none of the facilities and amenities enjoyed by the Chalet

School during its heyday. Nor did it have a glamorous alpine setting. And the teaching there was probably on the old-fashioned side, even for the times. On the other hand, there was in both schools a similar insistence on the importance of good manners and a disciplined attitude to work. But, at a guess, Elinor and her fellow pupils had a less exciting time than the Chalet girls!

(10) *What about the school Elinor ran in Hereford – was it at all like the Chalet School?*

Undoubtedly Elinor would have liked it to be. It seems, too, that she did attempt in the Margaret Roper School to foster the ideas of international co-operation and religious tolerance that had become familiar in the pages of the Chalet books. And clearly the basic aims and aspirations of the two schools had much in common. Another thing they shared was their school uniform, since Elinor deliberately chose one in brown and flame for the Hereford school, exactly similar in design to that worn at the Chalet School. The girls in Hereford also took part in many of the same activities as the Chalet girls, among them the annual Christmas play; and it even happened occasionally that the same play was given at both the fictional and the real-life schools. Nevertheless, although the Margaret Roper School was moderately successful for a time, it never came anywhere near the Chalet School's league. For one thing, Elinor, despite her love of children and genuine gifts as a teacher, was simply not cut out to be a headmistress. Miss Annersley would have had much to show her.

(11)   *Why is the spelling in the books sometimes TYROL and sometimes TIROL?*

The first of these – Tyrol with a "Y" – was for many years the standard English spelling of the word, and hence the one Elinor would probably have accepted without question at the time she began writing the Chalet School books. However, in Germany and Austria the spelling was always more commonly Tirol – with an "I", and more recently this latter spelling has been adopted in English also, being now considered more authentic. Elinor uses "Tyrol" consistently in the earlier stories, changing to "Tirol" somewhere around the twentieth story. (In this book, I have used "Tirol" and "Tirolean" except in any quotations where Elinor may have used the other form.)

(12)   *How old is Jo when the triplets are born?*

This is a more complicated question than it appears. In the paperback edition of *The Chalet School in Exile* (Chapter 13) Jo is stated to be nearly 21 when her three babies arrive. But the same chapter in the original hardback edition gives her age at the time as nearly 22. The latter would really be the more consistent; for if allowance is made for a year between the escape from Austria and the Chalet School's re-opening in Guernsey, then Jo would have to be nearly 22 in the November when her triplets are born, because it is clear she was already over 20 at the beginning of *The Chalet School in Exile*. That, at any rate, is the inference to be drawn from the ages of Robin Humphries and Peggy Bettany, who are 14 and 8 respectively at this point in the story – Joey having been 12, nearly 13, when the Robin was 6, and 14½ when Peggy was born. It would also allow time for the visit Jo paid to India, described in the missing book, *Two Chalet Girls in India* (see question (8) above). However, it seems that Elinor must definitely have wanted this particular change, for references in later books usually give Jo's age as 20 when her first babies were born.

(13)   *How many books are there altogether in the Chalet School series?*

Originally the series consisted of fifty-eight full-length stories in hardback and one shorter paperback, all published between 1925 and 1970 by W. & R. Chambers Ltd. But Nos 10, 13 and 35 of the original stories were divided for publication in Armada, and the second part of each was then retitled. As a result the total number of different titles is now sixty-two. There were also various books connected with the series, including three annuals and a book of recipes, and the two "missing" stories, mentioned above (Question (8)). For a complete list of titles see page 158.

(14) *What is the correct reading order for the stories? – is it the same as the order in which they were published originally?*

Most often this question is asked by readers who have come across the hardback edition of *Tom Tackles the Chalet School*, and cannot understand how this story fits into the series. Nor is this surprising; for suddenly in this book, which was theoretically No 31 of the hardback series, Tom Gay, of the title role, appears to have gone back several years and to have become a new girl at the school; whereas in *The Chalet School and Barbara*, the book published the *previous* year and officially No 30, Tom had already been a prefect and in her final school year! This confusion arose because, although *Tom Tackles the Chalet School* was not published in book form until 1955, the story was in fact written much earlier and had originally been serialised in two Chalet School annuals during the late 1940s. Hence the events in this story actually take place before even those in *Three Go to the Chalet School*, which is officially No 20 of the hardback series.

There has, too, been confusion over another title, *The Chalet School and Rosalie*, which was also published out of chronological order, and has been described elsewhere as "not part of the series". This description simply meant that *The Chalet School and Rosalie*, having appeared only in a small paperback edition (published 1951), was not considered part of the original hardback series. The book in fact supplies an essential part of the chronicle; its story continues that of *Tom Tackles the Chalet School*, and precedes by some years that of *Three Go to the Chalet School*.

There is a further title, now included with the new edition of *The Chalet School and Rosalie* (published in May 1994), called *The Mystery at the Chalet School*. Not a full-length story, it was first published in *The Chalet Book for Girls* in 1947. It is set during the Christmas term following *Gay Lambert at the Chalet School* (and the summer holiday described in *Jo to the Rescue*). It immediately precedes *Tom Tackles the Chalet School*, which takes place during the Easter term. The events of the following summer term are related in *The Chalet School and Rosalie*.

But apart from these, all the other books in the series appeared in chronological order; although the events related in hardback Nos 25 and 26 take place during the same term; not consecutively but, in different places, simultaneously.

(15) *What happened to a book called* The Chalet School Musician, *which is announced as "Coming Soon" in one of the older Armada paperbacks but never seems to have been published?*

Many people have been puzzled by this, but unfortunately there is no definite answer to the question. The one thing certain is that no story with the title *The Chalet School Musician*, either published or unpublished, has ever existed. A possible explanation might be that before publication of the second part of *A Genius at the Chalet School* (which was divided for the paperback edition) the title *The Chalet School Musician* could for a time have been considered, being then abandoned in favour of *The Chalet School Fête* – the title actually used. But there can be no proof, either way.

(16) *What is the best way to collect a complete set of the Chalet School books?*

Armada has now published most of the series in paperback. All may not be currently available but a varying selection is kept in print, and with a bit of patience it should be possible to acquire all of them. Anyone interested in obtaining the original hard-backs, should try searching at secondhand booksellers or in charity shops, where these books do turn up from time to time, although unfortunately their prices nowadays can sometimes be rather high.

(17) *Did Elinor Brent-Dyer ever visit Switzerland before writing the books that are set in the Bernese Oberland?*

The only pre-war visits Elinor made to Europe were those to Austria in 1924 and to Oberammergau in 1930. After the war she would have found it difficult to take a holiday abroad, since for many years she was tied by the demands of work, and of caring not only for her mother but for other elderly ladies who lived with them. So, although the answer cannot be an absolutely definite "No", it is unlikely that Elinor ever managed a visit to Switzerland. And making a setting for the Chalet School would have given her no problems: plenty of information was available to her in travel brochures and guide books. Her imagination supplied the rest.

(18) *Why is it that Joey, who is a Roman Catholic, can be godmother to her sister's daughter, Josette Russell, whereas Madge isn't allowed to be godmother to any of Joey's family?*

It is correct that Joey is Josette's godmother; and that she tells Madge at the time of the triplets' christening, " 'Sorry I can't have you [as godmother], my dear, but as they'll be brought up Catholics, it can't be done.' " But – for once – this is not as inconsistent as it may appear. Josette is at least a year older than the Maynard triplets, and at the time of her birth it is possible that Joey was still, like her elder sister, a member of the Church of England, which would explain the apparent discrepancy. It is never made clear at what point Jo did become a Roman Catholic; nor, for that matter why her husband should have been a Catholic at all, since his sister, Molly Maynard, is definitely C. of E. in all the early stories. But this is just part of the usual pattern!

(19) *Why are there so many inconsistencies in the Chalet School series?*

Even the most devoted fan could not deny that the Chalet books contain a luxuriant crop of inconsistencies. People change their names, their ages, their religious affiliations, and their occupations at a bewildering rate – and sometimes more than once. Place names can also change; and, even more disconcertingly, the places can sometimes remove themselves from, for example, one side of a mountain or valley to the other (as happens to the Bärenbad mountain in the ninth story). The head girl in one book is apparently demoted to being only library prefect in the next, while the roll of past head girls varies capriciously. And so on – and on . . . All readers will have their own pet list.

Perhaps the oddest change of name is the transformation of Elise La Pâttre into Thérèse Lepâttre, which – along with the tangle of Matrons, Lloyd/Gould/Rider – has already been discussed above. Another who suffers name changes is Molly Maynard: her married name appears in three different versions. Then Mary Burnett, the Chalet School's fifth head girl (Yes, that's *right*!) is described, when she's first mentioned, as being in a form *below* Joey at the High School they both attended in England; yet, when she arrives at the Chalet School only a term later, she has apparently aged three years, thus accounting for her becoming head girl while Jo is still barely sixteen. For that matter, the town of Taverton, where that High School was located and where the Bettanys are living in the early chapters of *The School at the Chalet*, is at one point in Cornwall, yet before long finds itself across the border in Devon (or was there perhaps a boundary change . . .?).

Among my own favourite inconsistencies is one that was pointed out by Miss Polly Goerres in her dissertation on "The Language, Traditions and Genre of the Chalet School Series". It concerns Clem Barras's temperamental artist father, who ends an outburst with the ringing declaration: "'And mark my words it will, or my name's not Adrian Charles Barras!'". And, lo and behold, four books later his name is NOT Adrian Charles Barras: he is now apparently Miles Barras, although at least he's still an artist.

Now, it is easy enough to point out the inconsistencies – it would be difficult to miss them in some cases; but, to try and explain why they arose in such profusion – that's quite another matter. The simple answer would be that Elinor Brent-Dyer had a poor memory and was an exceedingly unmethodical person. And this would be undeniable. But there are, nevertheless, points to be made in her defence. The writing of a series is a highly complicated affair. Those people, for example, who compile radio or television soap operas, have to keep the most careful records of all that takes place in the story, along with card indexes giving minute details of the characters – their ages, family backgrounds, appearance, occupation, etc., etc. And nowadays any writer contemplating a series, even one of moderate length, would have to approach the undertaking in this professional way. But in Elinor's day things were different, and school-story writers had a far more casual attitude. Besides, it must not be overlooked that when Elinor began the Chalet books she was not aiming specifically to write a series, let alone one of fifty-nine books (in the original numbering). Maybe she did intend to provide a few sequels to *The School at the Chalet*; but in the early stages she cannot have had the smallest notion of the enormous length her series would eventually reach. That said, it must be acknowledged that Elinor might not have organised things any better even if she had realised in advance the size of her undertaking. After all, she did manage in *Jo of the Chalet School* to describe Simone Lecoutier as Mademoiselle's *niece*, whereas in the previous book the two had been some kind of cousins. And this happens at a point when the series contains only the two books . . .

But far more interesting than the mere existence of all these flaws, is the quite extraordinary degree of tolerance that readers have shown towards them. Obviously they are not considered to be very important compared with other things – irritating at times, mildly amusing at others, and good occasionally for an hour or two's speculation in trying to sort them out. The readers' attitude recalls that taken by some families to a forgetful but well-liked relative: "Oh that's just Aunt So-and-So – she always gets things muddled; but she's the greatest fun!" And when all's said and done, Elinor does manage to keep her immense cast of characters behaving all through the stories with remarkable consistency. She may confuse their ages, and many other things about them; even at times their names. Never their personalities.

SHORT STORY

Joey Shoves her Oar In

"Backwater, Joey – quick! – Oh, *bother*!"

Miss Wilson was cross. Her pupil, obviously dreaming and forgetting not only where she was, but the very meaning of the term "backwater", made a sudden wild lunge with her oars, caught a large and complicated crab, and ended up on her back in the bottom of the boat, most of the breath knocked out of her. The other occupant wiped the wide grin off his face as he leant forward from the stern to heave the crowing Jo to a sitting position.

"Are you hurt?" he asked anxiously.

"Wa-ah – ha-ah! Just – winded!" gasped Jo.

"If you'd only remembered what I said, it wouldn't have happened," said Miss Wilson severely, as she left the steering to look after itself and, seizing one of Jo's forlornly trailing oars, tried hard to push off from the shingle-heap on which that young lady's exploit had grounded them.

"Allow me," said Dr Maynard, seeing that Jo was getting her breath back, and carefully moving over to where Miss Wilson was struggling against the yielding shingle without much result. "Get her head straight, will you? Now—" He thrust hard against the bottom, and the boat moved a little. Two or three more good shoves did it, and they were once more floating safely on the lake. Jo mopped her scarlet face with a handkerchief that had seen better days, and gasped until she had got her breath back.

Miss Wilson took no notice of her, for she felt very cross.

It was too bad! Only yesterday evening she had been boasting to the newly arrived Dr Maynard of the rowing prowess of the Chalet School girls, and of Jo Bettany in particular. He had smiled politely, and said how nice it was for the girls to get a little boating. But this whole attitude had also suggested that an Oxford Rowing Blue didn't expect much in that line from schoolgirls. It was with the idea of expelling this notion that the mistress had invited him and Jo Bettany to come for a row that afternoon. The rest of the school disported itself in the other two boats under the eye of Miss Nalder, the games mistress, or bathed and swam with some of the Staff on duty. And now Joey had let her down!

Jo knew quite well what Miss Wilson was thinking. She put her handkerchief away, pushed the thick black fringe of her hair out of her eyes, and said apologetically, "I'm awfully sorry, Miss Wilson!"

Miss Wilson's face did not relax. "I've told you before not to let your thoughts wander when you're in a boat," she said briefly.

"I know; I'm most awfully sorry."

138

Jo sounded so penitent that Miss Wilson gave in. "We'll say no more. But I shouldn't like to think what might happen if you were in a boat alone, Jo. Let her have the oars, Dr Maynard. She really can row quite well, though I admit her latest performance isn't calculated to make you think so."

Dr Maynard gave up the oars, and Joey, determined to retrieve her reputation, put her whole back into the task, sending the boat skimming across the mirror-like surface of the lake with long, steady strokes.

When Miss Wilson gave the word to return, the young doctor gave her a smiling nod.

"Yes, Jo can row well on occasion. I congratulate you on her style, Miss Wilson. But look here, young woman," and he swung round on Jo. "You must learn to keep your head. It's the last thing to lose when you're in a boat. Lose your oars, lose your rudder – if lose them you *must* – but lose your head, and you're probably lost yourself!"

"Not necessarily!" retorted Jo. "I *can* swim, you know."

"Can you indeed?" he exclaimed. "But if you lost your head, even swimming mightn't be much use to you."

They were nearing the shore by this time. The Tiernsee, loveliest of all Tirol's lovely lakes, is by no means large. The doctor glanced across at the other boats, which were also pulling in rather expertly.

"Good style!" he said to Miss Wilson. "I must say I admire your pupils."

They had reached the little landing-stage at this

point, where Hansi, boy-of-all-work at the school, was waiting to draw the boats in. The doctor sprang out and offered his hand first to Miss Wilson and then to Jo. But Jo's "back was up". She ignored the hand, jumped lightly ashore, and turned away, leaving the mistress surrounded by eager claimants for the next turn in the boats, and stalked off to the school garden, where she sought a certain large chestnut tree and flung herself into a deck-chair in the shade. Here she sprawled, comfortably if inelegantly, for the next twenty minutes, scowling blackly into the distance, and thinking things not lawful to be uttered. She was roused from this unpraiseworthy occupation by Matron, who happened to pass by and saw her.

"Jo Bettany!" she exclaimed in horrified tones. "If you have finished with the boats, go and make yourself fit to be seen."

"Yes, Matron," said Jo sulkily as she got to her feet, and went off to the house. "Oh, *hang*!" she thought, making her way to her cubicle. "I do wish people would let people alone!"

However, when she was washed and dressed in a clean frock, her gollywog mop brushed smooth, she had to admit that she felt better. She went back to the garden, where she found her own special coterie of friends congregated by the chestnut, awaiting her. The usual afternoon refection of Kaffee und Kuchen had been brought out, and by degrees Jo began to feel soothed, though she was not yet ready to forgive the doctor for having seen her make "a complete noodle of herself" as she phrased it.

It was Saturday, so there was no evening preparation to worry about, and as it was a very hot day, there would be no dancing either that night. The girls carried their used crockery to the kitchens, and then settled down in the shadiest spots they could find to gossip about school affairs, read, or sew, or write letters.

Grizel Cochrane, head-girl of the school, presently sauntered to the various groups to say that Mademoiselle, the Head of the school, had given permission for all those of fifteen or over to go for a walk after Abendessen, provided they were back at twenty-one o'clock (nine, by English time), and it had been decided to stroll along to a little hamlet about a couple of miles up the lake known as Gaisalm.

"Any of the staff coming?" asked Jo.

"No. If it gets cool enough, they want to get a little tennis," said Grizel. "We prefects will be in charge."

"Well, that's rather good for a change. I quite like our Staff, but it makes a nice break to go off by ourselves once in a way," said Jo thoughtfully. "By the way, Grizel, can we take our purses with us? Old Lisa may be about, and I'd like some fruit."

"I expect so. I'll go and ask, though. Lisa might have apricots, so it's a good idea," said Grizel, going off to seek the required permission.

Mademoiselle readily agreed to the idea. "Do not let them buy too much," she said. "Matron will not wish to sit up all night with girls who are sick from eating too much fruit, as you know, mon chou."

Grizel promised that she and the other prefects

141

would keep an eye on the younger ones, and went back to spread the glad news, while Joey and Co., reassured on this point, settled back in their chairs and continued with their idle chatter.

After Abendessen and Prayers, while the tinies went to bed, and while those under fifteen scattered about the gardens and the playing-fields to make the most of what time was left them, the elder girls set out. They had to go in double file as long as they were in Briesau, the little lake village where the school was situated, for, apart from the chalets where the inhabitants lived, there were several large hotels which were rapidly filling up now, and no one wanted to give strangers anything but a good impression of the school.

They looked very fresh and charming in their summer frocks and big hats, walking demurely down the lake-path, and the visitors sitting on the verandah of the Kron Prinz Karl Hotel near the lake-steamer landing-stage, or on the seats set here and there by the lake, commented approvingly on them as they went past. Once they were beyond the white fence which divides Briesau from the narrow path leading to Gaisalm, however, they broke file, and strolled along in little knots of three or four, enjoying the evening breeze from the lake, and their tongues going busily.

Joey and her three friends, Marie von Eschenau, Frieda Mensch, and Simone Lecoutier, were in advance of the rest. As they turned a curve in the path, they came upon a small girl of eight or nine who was lying at full length on the grassy bank that ran up here between the lower path and an upper one. This upper path was none too safe, and the girls never took it unless a mistress was with them.

As they advanced, this small person suddenly rolled over on to her face, keeping her head with its masses of silky fair tangles bent down as if she were deeply interested in something in the grass. But the sharp eyes of the four had seen that her face was tear-stained – also dirty – and her eyes were red. Also, besides the fact that her hair would have been the better for a good brushing, her frock was badly soiled and crumpled.

"I wonder what is wrong?" murmured Marie von Eschenau in the Tirolean German which was second nature to all of them. "Should we ask, do you think?"

"She probably wouldn't say and mightn't understand, for one thing. Anyhow, it looks as if she meant to ignore us," said Joey, casting a glance at the blue back so firmly turned on them.

"Is she a visitor?" asked Frieda.

"Well, as she's no one I've ever seen before, I should think that was the most likely," returned Jo. "I should like to hear Matey's remarks about her frock. Did you ever see such a mess? Anyhow," she wound up virtuously, "it's far too late for a babe like that to be up. She ought to have been in bed half an hour ago!"

They were past her by this time, and also past the grassy slopes. Now the path was of naked rock, running along above the lake, with a sheer drop down to the water, and a steep slope up to the upper path, which went on rising till there were some twenty feet or more between them. Along they went and presently came to one of the show-places of the lake-side, a great overhanging rock from which trickled a stream of water that rose from one of the hillside springs. It dripped on to another rocky platform, beneath which the ground sloped down to the lake, where the tiny rill, flowing through the narrow channel it had cut for itself, entered the lake waters. If there had been rain, the Dripping Rock was a sight to behold. But tonight there was only the one little stream, though the face of the rock was never really dry.

Sitting on a boulder at one side was old Lisa, the fruit-woman, with a great hamper of ripe apricots beside her, and the four were soon so busy chaffering with her that all thought of the little stranger passed out of their heads. They finally got what they wanted, by which time the rest had come up, and they too thronged round Lisa. She did a brisk trade until her hamper was empty, and she was able to trot home with a pocketful of small silver, and a heart rejoicing that her little garden was the sunniest and most sheltered one in the district. Her fruit was always ripe at least a fortnight before her neighbours'; and by this she profited.

The girls, after bidding the old lady "Grüss Gott", stood for a moment, eating apricots, and comparing the stream from the rock with its appearance in flood, when an anxious-looking woman, unmistakably English, came hurrying along the path from Gaisalm. She saw the girls and stopped.

"Can we help you?" asked Grizel, taking the lead as head-girl.

"Oh, praise 'Eaven you speaks English!" ejaculated the woman. "'Ave you seen a little girl, Miss? Blue frock and fair 'air?"

Grizel shook her head. "We've seen nothing—" she was beginning, when Jo "butted in". "*We* saw her – lying on the bank a bit nearer Briesau, where the upper path begins the sharp rise. A dirty cotton frock, and a perfect mop of fair hair. Is that her?"

"Sounds like 'er, though that frock was clean at tea-time."

"Jo, are you sure?" asked Grizel. "There was no child anywhere about when we came past."

"She was there all right," said Jo. "Wasn't she, you three?"

They hastened to back her up. "She was certainly there, Grizel," said Marie. "We all saw her."

"Perhaps she climbed up the bank to the upper path," suggested Simone.

"I hope not!" cried Frieda. "It isn't safe! You know that!"

"Not safe?" cried the woman. "Oh, Miss—"

"I'll tell you," said Jo quickly. "We're going on to Gaisalm. Some of us had better go up the path from there to where the grass and bushes begin again. Grizel, you and the others could run back, get up by the grassy slope, and come along so far. We can take—" She paused doubtfully, and looked at the woman.

"My name's Price, Miss. I'm 'er ladyship's maid, and 'ave charge of Miss Georgiana while 'er nurse is away. And a nice 'andful she is! Won't do a thing she's bid, and most of the time 'er ladyship just laughs at 'er naughty ways. But she'll 'ave plenty to say if she thinks on to ask for 'er and she ain't there!"

"Well," said Jo briskly, paying no heed to this diatribe, "you come back with us."

She was interrupted by a cry from Price. "Miss Georgiana – Miss Georgiana! You bad little gel! What will 'er ladyship say when she 'ears 'ow you've been be'aving?"

The girls all looked up to the top of the rock, where a little figure stood, halted in mid-path by the maid's cry.

"Come down at once, Miss!" urged Price.

Georgiana set her hands on her hips and looked down. "I won't," she said with finality. "You're only making a fuss 'cos you think Aunt Evelyn will be mad if I'm not there if she asks for me. I like it up here, and I'm not coming down for hours and hours yet, so it's no good you talking, Price!"

Price wrung her hands. "Oh, you bad little gel! Come down at once, Miss Georgiana! Do you 'ear me?"

"I should think they hear you all over the lake!" retorted Georgiana. "I'm not coming, I told you." And she stepped to the edge of the rock to sit down.

Grizel took a hand. She knew how dangerous the slippery rock was. "Get back, you little ass!" she ordered in her best head-girl manner. "D'you want to be killed? Get back!"

Slightly overawed, Georgiana stepped back, and

her foot slipped. Price uttered a shrill scream, but luckily the child managed to save herself. She dropped on all fours, crawled back from the edge, and crouched down. Grizel held a hasty council with the others and then addressed Price.

"Make your way to Gaisalm and wait. Some of us will go back to get Georgiana, and bring her to you by this path." Raising her voice, she called: "Georgiana!"

"Ye-ye-es?" came in shaky tones. Georgiana had been scared by that narrow escape.

"Stay where you are, and we'll come and get you. It isn't safe for you up there. The rocks get worse over the next bit, and you might take a nasty toss. Promise you'll do as I say."

"I'll stay."

Grizel turned to the others. "Rosalie, you and Gertrud come with me, and we'll climb up and get her. The rest go on to Gaisalm and wait there for us. We shan't be long. Take Price with you. That babe's all right so long as she keeps still, and we'll get her quickly."

Price was unnerved by her charge's narrow escape. She went with the girls quite meekly, while the three prefects went racing back the way they had come to ascend to the upper path by the grassy slope. All would have been well if Georgiana had not suddenly realised that she was being left alone, and completely lost her head. With a cry she sprang up, tried to run level with the rest, caught her foot on a projecting fragment of rock, and, with a scream that none of them forgot, went clean over the edge. Mercifully,

147

in her efforts to regain her balance, she had flung herself outwards, so she did not land on the rocky path below, or there would have been a tragedy. Instead, she cleared it, and plunged heavily into the ice-cold waters of the lake, extra chilly at this part, owing to the under-water springs.

With a yell, Jo sprang to the edge, but was caught and held back by Mary Burnett, the second prefect, who cried, "You can't go after her, Jo! It's too icy!"

"Clausen's boat!" said Jo, with a wriggle which tore the sleeve out of her frock and set her free.

She took advantage of the second before Mary could grasp her again to drop neatly and accurately into a broad-beamed boat moored to a ring in the rock below, and Marie, one of the best oars in the school, followed her. With bated breath, the rest watched the pair wrench loose the knot which held the boat. Then Jo, working as fast as she could, pushed out the oars, and gently moved the boat out, while Marie, kneeling in the bows, searched the cold blue waters for a sign of Georgiana.

The little fair head came to the surface not far away, and the watchers saw the child essay a feeble stroke or two. Then the boat hid her from view. Marie was leaning perilously over the side while Jo, trailing her oars, flung her weight the other way to make the boat trim.

"Get her to the bows, Marie," they heard her shout. "We can't pull her over the side. She's too heavy."

She gripped the oar, and backwatered very gently, bringing the bows of the boat level with Georgiana, who was numbed by the chill of the water and made no effort to help herself. Then Jo shipped her oars, and joined Marie. There were two or three hair-raising moments for those on shore before they saw the two girls gradually drag the child into the boat, where she finally rolled at their feet, limp and still.

For a moment or two neither moved, so spent were they. Then, very cautiously, Jo wriggled back to her place at the oars, unshipped them, and, pulling wearily, got the boat back, bringing it to the platform below the Dripping Rock.

By the time they reached there, the other girls were waiting, and while a prefect steadied the boat, Mary and Deira, sturdy seventeen-year-olds, got in and lifted out the still little heap that was Georgiana, whereupon Price, who had never ceased to wail and wring her hands, flopped down in a faint beside them.

They left her to recover as best she could. Mary and Deira stripped off the wet clothes, and rubbed Georgiana till the blue look left her face and she was breathing more strongly. Then they wrapped her in the undergarments some of the others had hastily discarded. She was lifted and laid on a hurriedly improvised stretcher made by four girls locking hands, and borne as quickly as they dared along the path to Gaisalm. Jo and Marie had been ministered to by their clan, and Grizel and the others, who had turned back on hearing Price scream, formed up and helped them along.

They reached the Gasthaus, which is the main building at Gaisalm, and saw a pretty lady laughing and chattering gaily with some other people under a tree. The chatter broke off short as the party arrived. Then the lady recognised the fair hair, uttered a cry, and came tearing over the green turf to them.

Georgiana was borne off to hot drinks, bath, and bed, and the girls were made to sit down and drink big cups of coffee, which they needed by this time. The lady, still looking distraught, came out of the Gasthaus to tell them that her little niece was asleep, and seemed to have taken no harm. By this time poor Price had made her appearance, moaning and sobbing with the shock. All in all, it was an exciting time.

Frieda, always thoughtful, slipped into the Gasthaus to ring up the school and explain that they might be late, and what had happened. The rest learned by degrees that the lady was Lady Todd, and Georgiana was her brother's child, who had been left in her charge while he and his wife were away on a trip to the West Indies. The child was badly spoiled, and Lady Todd, bored with the care of a tiresome small girl of nine, had left her very much in the hands of Nanny. To pass the time, she had brought the young lady with her on this trip to Tirol. Nanny had been summoned home, and Price was supposed to look after the child. As for Georgiana's earlier tears, Lady Todd's party had arranged for a moonlight trip on the lake, and the child wanted to go with them. Her aunt flatly refused, and she had gone off in a rage. Hence all this trouble!

It was very late when the girls finally got back, but not much was said. The "saying" came next day, from Miss Wilson to Dr Maynard, when she told him the story, and made him acknowledge that girls could row as well as boys. Her girls had shown in particular that they did indeed know how to manage a boat *and* keep their heads. She was fully justified in her boasts about Jo Bettany.

HURRAY FOR THE CHALET SCHOOL!

Chalet Fans Past and Present

"I have always wanted you to know how much I loved your books and what they meant to me . . . I was a complete Chalet girl, and could have recited your books by heart when I was young. I just lived for the next one to be published."

"I would like to express my enjoyment of the Chalet School series, of which I have read all thirty-three . . . I hope you are going to write some more in the series, as I think the people are alive and real and I know all about them . . . I have just read *The Chalet School Goes to It* for the umpteenth time, today. In 'forbidden slang', I think your books are 'smashing'."

"Apart from some of the expressions they use, like 'top-hole', I always think of the Chalet School as happening today."

The writers quoted above appear to be at one, and certainly they are united in their enthusiasm for the

Chalet books. Nevertheless, they represent three widely spaced generations. The first letter, although written in 1979, refers to schooldays more than fifty years earlier, in the 1920s. The second expresses the opinion in 1956 of a fifteen-year-old fan in Newcastle-upon-Tyne. The third was written in the late 1980s by an Aberdeen schoolgirl who was twelve at the time. Thus the three letters – and several hundred others exist – span between them more than sixty years of "Chaletomania".

There are of course many different ways for new readers to arrive at the Chalet School, and there are Chalet fans of all ages. It is interesting, possibly surprising, to note too that the Chalet books, judging not only by current paperback sales but also by the countless fan letters received, are as popular today as they were in the Twenties and Thirties, and not just with children. Fans come from many different countries, and from various social backgrounds (although for obvious reasons the majority are British, and admittedly more of them than not are middle class). Some have attended boarding schools, others not; several today are pupils at large comprehensives; some have travelled abroad and may have studied foreign languages; some have done neither. Many did meet the Chalet stories during childhood, but a sizeable minority did not. A few continue to read the books with uncritical admiration; some lose interest altogether, but many more of all ages go on enjoying the stories despite being aware of their flaws. Chalet School readers cannot be put into any one category.

One thing that is shared by most fans in every age group is an intense interest in the Chalet School characters, whose quasi reality seems often to be taken for granted in fan letters. For example (and it should be borne in mind that all correspondents are writing to someone who was a complete stranger):

One grown-up fan, discussing two possible courses of action, wrote – and only half-jokingly – "I am sure no true Chalet girl would do the latter."

Another related how at Christmas-time – "and this has been in Japan, the USA, and once going up the Suez Canal", she is often "far away, walking down the mountain path to Spärtz . . . having coffee in the station waiting room with Herr Anserl . . . setting out with Madge, Jo and the Robin to visit the Mensch family in Innsbruck".

A third finished her letter: "Although we have never met, I feel we already have a link as friends of the Bettany and Maynard families."

The last writer clearly considered herself one of the Chalet School's extended family, and there is no doubt that fans attach great importance to this notion of belonging to a group. At one time – from May 1959 to September 1969 – there existed the original Chalet School Club, which enjoyed a growth rate not unlike that of the fictional school itself: in the course of the first five years the membership rose from an initial thirty-three to just under four thousand, and it remained at around this level for a further five years, when the club had to be disbanded following Elinor's death. It is worth stressing, too, that it was not during the heyday of the school story that this Chalet Club existed. Had there been such a club during the Twenties or Thirties it would not have been so astonishing, for the school story was then high fashion. That the Chalet Club was a going concern as recently as 1969 underlines what is probably the most remarkable feature of the series: the way in which, despite changing fashions, its popularity endures, right up to the present day.

In further and striking testimony to this, two new Chalet School clubs have been launched during the past few years. First in the field were The Friends of the Chalet School – this club began in Australia in 1988, but expanded so rapidly that the organisation now has to be shared by a committee of four – three in the UK and one in Australia. The ever-increasing membership includes fans from nine different countries. A second group, The Chaletian, was founded more recently in Britain, but already has members throughout the country, and was able in 1992 to organise a group visit to the Tirol. Both clubs produce their own regular.magazines (information available from Armada).

One way and another, if things continue as they do at present, there seems no reason why the Chalet School should not continue to flourish for a very long time indeed.

COMPLETE LIST OF TITLES IN
THE CHALET SCHOOL SERIES

Originally the series consisted of fifty-eight full-length stories in hardback and one shorter paperback, all published by W. & R. Chambers Ltd. But Nos 10, 13 and 35 of the original stories were divided for publication in paperback by Armada, and the second part of each was then retitled (see below). The following is a complete list of the series, dated in order of original publication. The number given to Armada editions is shown in brackets. All the titles in the series, with the exception of those given in italics and the books only connected with the series (viz. the annuals and cookbook) have been published by Armada, though all may not currently be in print.

An up-to-date stocklist is available on request from Armada, HarperCollins Publishers Ltd, 77–85 Fulham Palace Road, London W6 8JB.

1. (1) The School at the Chalet – 1925
2. (2) Jo of the Chalet School – 1926
3. (3) The Princess of the Chalet School – 1927
4. (4) The Head Girl of the Chalet School – 1928

5. (5)   Rivals of the Chalet School – 1929
6. (6)   Eustacia Goes to the Chalet School – 1930
7. (7)   The Chalet School and Jo – 1931
8. (8)   The Chalet Girls in Camp – 1932
9. (9)   Exploits of the Chalet Girls – 1933
10. The Chalet School and the Lintons – 1934
    Published in two Armada volumes:
    (10)   The Chalet School and the Lintons
    (11)   A Rebel at the Chalet School
11. (12)   The New House at the Chalet School – 1935
12. (13)   Jo Returns to the Chalet School – 1936
13. The New Chalet School – 1938
    Published in two Armada volumes:
    (14)   The New Chalet School
    (15)   A United Chalet School
14. (16)   The Chalet School in Exile – 1940
15. (17)   The Chalet School at War – 1941
    (*original title* The Chalet School Goes To It)
16. (18)   The Highland Twins at the Chalet School – 1942
17. (19)   Lavender Leigh at the Chalet School – 1943
    (*original title* Lavender Laughs in the Chalet School)
18. (20)   Gay Lambert at the Chalet School – 1944
    (*original title* Gay from China at the Chalet School)
19. (21)   *Jo to the Rescue* – 1945
    (22)   Tom Tackles the Chalet School – 1949
    (23)   The Chalet School and Rosalie – 1951 –

41.	(45)	Trials for the Chalet School – 1959
42.	(46)	Theodora and the Chalet School – 1959
43.	(47)	*Joey and Co. in Tirol* – 1960
44.	(48)	Ruey Richardson at the Chalet School – 1960
		(*original title* Ruey Richardson: Chaletian)
45.	(49)	A Leader in the Chalet School – 1961
46.	(50)	The Chalet School Wins the Trick – 1961
47.	(51)	*A Future Chalet School Girl* – 1962
48.	(52)	The Feud in the Chalet School – 1962
49.	(53)	The Chalet School Triplets – 1963
50.	(54)	*The Chalet School Reunion* – 1963
51.	(55)	Jane and the Chalet School – 1964
52.	(56)	Redheads at the Chalet School – 1964
53.	(57)	Adrienne and the Chalet School – 1965
54.	(58)	Summer Term at the Chalet School – 1965
55.	(59)	Challenge for the Chalet School – 1966
56.	(60)	Two Sams at the Chalet School – 1967
57.	(61)	Althea Joins the Chalet School – 1969
58.	(62)	Prefects of the Chalet School – 1970

Other books connected with the series:

The Chalet Book for Girls – 1947
The Second Chalet Book for Girls – 1948
The Third Chalet Book for Girls – 1949
(*The Mystery at the Chalet School* was published in the first book. *Tom Tackles the Chalet School* was serialised in the second and third books.)

The Chalet Girls' Cookbook – 1953

A book about Elinor Brent-Dyer and the Chalet School series, *Behind the Chalet School* by Helen McClelland, was published by New Horizon in 1981. It is still available from public libraries in many parts of the country.